Campaign • 178

The Rhine Crossings 1945

Ken Ford • Illustrated by Howard Gerrard

First published in Great Britain in 2006 by Osprey Publishing, Midland House, West Way, Botley, Oxford OX2 0PH, United Kindgom.
443 Park Avenue South, New York, NY 10016, USA.
Email: info@ospreypublishing.com

A CIP catalogue record for this book is available from the British Library

ISBN 978 1 84603 026 0

The author, Ken Ford, has asserted his right under the Copyright, Designs and Patents Act, 1988, to be identified as the Author of this Work.

Design: The Black Spot
Index: Alison Worthington
Maps by The Map Studio
Typeset in Helvetica Neue and ITC New Baskerville
3d bird's-eye views by The Black Spot
Battlescene artwork by Howard Gerrard
Originated by United Graphics Ltd, Singapore
Printed in China through Worldprint

07 08 09 10 11   10 9 8 7 6 5 4 3 2 1

For a catalogue of all books published by Osprey please contact:
Osprey Direct UK, PO Box 140, Wellingborough,
Northants, NN8 2FA, UK
Email: info@ospreydirect.co.uk

North America
Osprey Direct, c/o Random House Distribution Center,
400 Hahn Road, Westminster, MD 21157
Email: info@ospreydirect.co.uk

www.ospreypublishing.com

Artist's note

Readers may care to note that the original paintings from which the color plates in this book were prepared are available for private sale. All reproduction copyright whatsoever is retained by the Publishers. All inquiries should be addressed to:

Howard Gerrard
11 Oaks Road
Tenterden
Kent
TN30 6RD
UK

The Publishers regret that they can enter into no correspondence upon this matter.

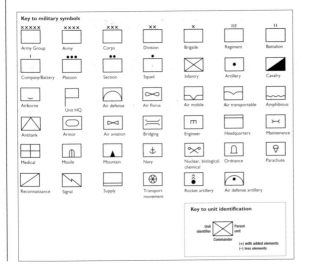

CONTENTS

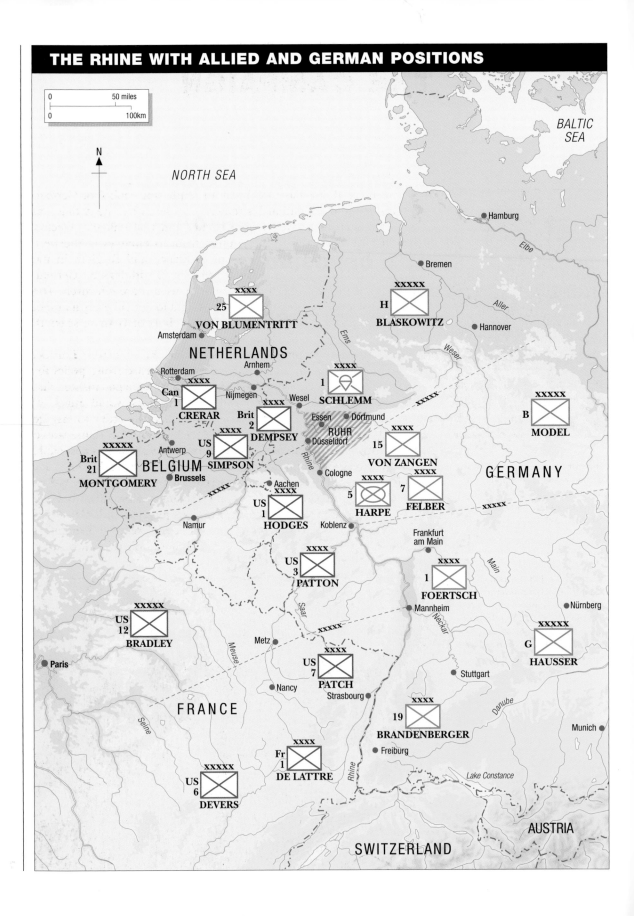

THE RHINE WITH ALLIED AND GERMAN POSITIONS

BALTIC SEA

NORTH SEA

Hamburg

Elbe

Bremen

Aller

XXXXX

H BLASKOWITZ

Hannover

Weser

25 VON BLUMENTRITT

Amsterdam

NETHERLANDS

Rotterdam

Arnhem

Nijmegen

Ems

1 SCHLEMM

XXXXX

B MODEL

GERMANY

Can 1 CRERAR

Wesel

Essen Dortmund

RUHR

XXXXX

Brit 2 DEMPSEY

Düsseldorf

15 VON ZANGEN

Brit 21 MONTGOMERY

Antwerp

US 9 SIMPSON

Cologne

BELGIUM

Brussels

5 HARPE

7 FELBER

Aachen

US 1 HODGES

Koblenz

Namur

Frankfurt am Main

1 FOERTSCH

US 3 PATTON

US 12 BRADLEY

Saar

Mannheim

Neckar

Nürnberg

Paris

Meuse

Metz

US 7 PATCH

G HAUSSER

Nancy

Stuttgart

Strasbourg

FRANCE

Seine

19 BRANDENBERGER

Danube

Munich

Freiburg

Fr 1 DE LATTRE

Rhine

Lake Constance

US 6 DEVERS

SWITZERLAND

AUSTRIA

0 — 50 miles
0 — 100km

N

ORIGINS OF THE CAMPAIGN

A paratrooper from 6th Airborne Division ready for action on the eastern side of the River Rhine during Operation *Varsity*. (BU 2561, IWM)

Troops of the 9th Durham Light Infantry from 131st Infantry Brigade in a Kangaroo armoured personnel carrier. The brigade was the infantry arm of the 7th Armoured Division, the Desert Rats. (BU 2847, IWM)

The River Rhine has long been an important symbol of German history and of national strength – a defensive moat that was often seen as a psychological barrier and vital military objective separating the heartland of the country from its enemies in the west. After the Allied invasion and the fall of France and Belgium in the autumn of 1944, Hitler's generals urged him to withdraw all German forces behind the river where they might be used more effectively. The Führer refused and insisted that his troops fight to defend every metre of soil, a policy which eventually resulted in the bulk of German strength being destroyed west of the Rhine.

The Supreme Commander of Allied Forces in north-west Europe, Gen Dwight D. Eisenhower, had implemented a 'broad front' policy for the advance of his forces from France into Germany. He had insisted that his Canadian, British, American and French armies would attack all along the line from the North Sea to Switzerland in order to engage German forces everywhere they could. Attacks across the Rhine would only be launched when all of his forces were lined up along its west bank.

By March 1945 Eisenhower's armies were at the River Rhine, ready for the assault. In the north was FM Bernard Montgomery's Twenty-First Army Group, with Gen Harry Crerar's Canadian First Army holding the left of the line from the North Sea to its junction with Gen Miles Dempsey's British Second Army near Xanten. Next to Dempsey's formation, just south of Wesel, was Gen Bill Simpson's US Ninth Army.

British medium guns join in the pre-assault artillery bombardment of the German side of the Rhine, part of the covering fire put down by almost 3,500 Allied guns. (BU 2143, IWM)

South of Montgomery's army group was Gen Omar Bradley's US Twelfth Army Group with Gen Hodges' US First Army on the left between Cologne and Koblenz and Gen George Patton's US Third Army on the right holding the river up to Mannheim. All of these formations had advanced to the Rhine from the beaches of Normandy. Farther south, the line was held by Gen Jacob Dever's US Sixth Army Group which had come north from the landings on the French Riviera. Gen Patch's US Seventh Army was taking up position along the Rhine south of Mannheim to Strasbourg, with Gen de Lattre's French First Army holding the remainder of the river up to the Swiss border.

Gen Eisenhower had stuck to his broad-front strategy in spite of often quite virulent criticism from the commander of British Twenty-First Army Group. FM Montgomery favoured the policy of the maximum use of force on a narrow front aimed at the industrial heartland of the Third Reich, which was situated in the north-western part of Germany. This northern front was also the most obvious direction to take into the heart of the country towards its capital Berlin. Whilst there was much military logic to commend Montgomery's proposal of applying the overwhelming use of power against a relatively small area of enemy resistance along the most favourable route, political considerations made it unacceptable.

Eisenhower had to consider the pride and sensibilities of all the fighting nations, most especially those of the USA who were providing the bulk of men and *matériel* to the campaign. All had to be fully involved in the drive for victory and Montgomery's plan would have geographical constraints which would make the drive into Germany mainly a British campaign. This would leave the cream of American forces to play a subsidiary role in the final downfall of Germany. Public opinion in the US, and military commanders on the ground, would not stand for this. Eisenhower chose to employ all of his strength in concert, pushing the Nazi forces back as they advanced. History has vindicated this policy, for it resulted in ultimate victory. Historians will, however, continue to argue whether or not the war could have been ended sooner, or indeed whether or not it might have taken longer, if a policy other than Eisenhower's had been adopted.

Gen Eisenhower did nonetheless agree that the main effort across the River Rhine would be made in the north, with Montgomery continuing to have the assistance of US Ninth Army under his command for the operation. The main reason for this was the proximity of the great industrial area of the Ruhr 40km to the south-east of Twenty-First Army Group's intended crossing places. This vast complex, 80km wide and 90km deep, was the only remaining powerhouse of Hitler's Third Reich – the industrial zones of Silesia and the Saar had already been overrun by the Russians and the Americans. It was essential that the Ruhr zone be captured to cut off Germany's last source of production. With US Ninth Army crossing under Montgomery in the north, and Gen Hodges' US First Army crossing farther south between Düsseldorf and Cologne, the Ruhr could be eliminated in a giant pincer movement by these two armies and might well precipitate a complete German collapse.

The problem of crossing the River Rhine had been carefully studied by Allied planners for a considerable time. Back in September of the previous year, Montgomery had unsuccessfully tried to get troops across the lower stretches of the river at Arnhem in Holland with an elaborate airborne operation. After this had failed serious thought had to be given to organizing another large-scale set-piece attack across the Rhine in northern Germany. By November 1944, an outline plan for the assault had been evolved. This was to be put into operation immediately after the area west of the river, the Rhineland, had been cleared. (See Campaign 74: *Rhineland 1944*)

These moves were delayed in late December 1944 when Hitler launched a counteroffensive through the Ardennes. All of Eisenhower's plans for any further advance into Germany were put on hold whilst Montgomery and Bradley's army groups dealt with the attack. The enemy threat was finally eliminated at the end of January 1945 and the

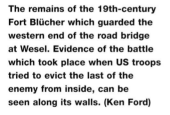

The remains of the 19th-century Fort Blücher which guarded the western end of the road bridge at Wesel. Evidence of the battle which took place when US troops tried to evict the last of the enemy from inside, can be seen along its walls. (Ken Ford)

front stabilized enough for the advance to continue. Montgomery then resumed his plans to clear the Rhineland prior to an assault across the river by British Second Army.

He launched an attack through the Reichswald Forest, Operation *Veritable*, on 8 February with Canadian First Army. After much bitter fighting, the Rhine was reached at Wesel on 10 March. Montgomery also cleared the area to the south of the Canadians with US Ninth Army in Operation *Grenade* to complete Twenty-First Army Group's move up to the Rhine. Enemy resistance to these moves was fierce, but the continued pressure being applied all along the line was irresistible and the subsequent fighting inflicted a costly defeat on the enemy. Gen der Fallschirmtruppen Alfred Schlemm's German First Parachute Army and Gen der Infanterie Gustav von Zangen's German Fifteenth Army were forced to retreat in some disorder back across the Rhine.

Gen Bradley continued his advance to the river in Operation *Lumberjack*. US First and Third Armies pushed their way through the German Fifth Panzer Army of Gen der Panzertruppen Hasso von Manteuffel and the German Seventh Army, commanded by Gen der Infanterie Hans Felber, in front of the Rhine. Calls to Hitler by these generals and their superiors to be allowed to retire back across the river in front of the Allied onslaught were denied, forcing C-in-C West, GenFM von Rundstedt, to waste his dwindling resources in a futile attempt to preserve a rapidly disintegrating front line.

Farther to the south, Gen Dever's US Sixth Army Group was pitting itself against Gen der Infanterie Hermann Foertsch's German First Army and Gen der Panzertruppen Hermann Balck's German Nineteenth Army. Outflanked by progress in the north and unable to halt the inexorable advance of US Seventh and French First Armies, these, too, were forced back across the upper Rhine.

One by one the enemy blew his bridges across the river as the Allies approached. He then tried to regroup his forces to resist the inevitable assault crossings. All the bridges were destroyed as planned bar one. By a stroke of good fortune the rail bridge at Remagen was captured intact, but damaged, by Hodges' US First Army. Gen Bradley sought permission from Eisenhower to put troops across and establish a bridgehead. The enemy side of the river was not the best type of terrain on which to conduct a powerful advance, but the psychological nature of the achievement was a great boost to the Allies. Eisenhower gave the go-ahead and the Rhine barrier was breached. Other crossings were soon to follow.

In stark contrast to Montgomery's intended set-piece and overwhelmingly strong plans to cross in the north, the Americans chose to improvise their crossings as chance allowed and to exploit any tactical situation on the far side of the river as it occurred. They had columns of engineers and

American troops move through a small German town during Operation *Grenade*, US Ninth Army's drive through the Rhineland to the River Rhine itself. (KY 54468, IWM)

Prime Minister Winston Churchill watches the airborne fly-in from a vantage point near the Rhine. With the premier, from left to right: Gen Crerar (Commander Canadian First Army), FM Alanbrooke (Chief of the Imperial General Staff), Lt Gen Simmonds (Commander Canadian II Corps) and FM Montgomery (Commander Twenty-First Army Group). (Barney J. Gloster/Dept. National Defence/National Archives of Canada, PA-143952).

bridging material just behind their front and troops ready to carry out an immediate assault. When US Third Army's commander, Gen George Patton, heard that his XII Corps was close to the river just south of Mainz, he ordered its commander, Gen Manton Eddy, to try to take the Rhine on the run. Gen S. Leroy Irwin's US 5th Division rose to the occasion and carried out a successful assault crossing on the same night as its 23rd Infantry Regiment arrived on the river. Now both US First and Third Armies had crossings over the Rhine before Montgomery was able to launch his long-awaited attack on the night of 23 March. It was with great glee that the anglophobic Gen George Patton was able to announce just before Montgomery's massive set-piece assault: 'Without the benefit of aerial bombardment, ground smoke, artillery preparations or airborne assistance, US Third Army at 2200hrs, Thursday evening 22nd March, crossed the Rhine.'

CHRONOLOGY

1944

17 September FM Montgomery launches Operation *Market Garden* in an attempt to cross the Lower Rhine at Arnhem.

25 September Operation *Market Garden* is abandoned when paratroopers are unable to hold on to their airborne bridgehead over the Rhine at Arnhem. The remnants of British 1st Airborne Division are withdrawn across the lower Rhine that night.

November Detailed planning begins for new crossings over the Rhine between Emerich and Rheinberg, timed to take place once the Rhineland to the west of the river is cleared of the enemy.

16 December Hitler launches a major offensive through the Ardennes which catches US First Army by surprise and drives deep into American territory. Planning for the Rhine crossing is delayed for a month while this bulge in the Allied line is removed.

20 December US Ninth Army placed under operational control of British Twenty-First Army Group to deal with the northern flank of Hitler's Ardennes offensive.

1945

February Ninth Army remains under the command of British Twenty-First Army Group for the Rhineland battle.

8 February Canadian First Army launches Operation *Veritable* to clear the Reichswald area of the Rhineland.

23 February US Ninth Army launches Operation *Grenade* to cross the River Roer and clear the Rhineland on the right flank of Canadian First Army.

7 March US III Corps captures the bridge over the River Rhine at Remagen and US First Army establishes a bridgehead across the river.

8 March The capture of a bridge over the Rhine is too much for Hitler and he decides to relieve GenFM von Rundstedt of his command and appoint GenFM Albert Kesselring as Commander-in-Chief (West).

American paratroopers from US XVIII Airborne Corps hitch a ride on the back of a British Churchill tank from 6th Guards Brigade. (FOX 60432, IWM)

The last planning stage before the Rhine airborne operation: from left to right, Grp Capt R.C. Sutcliffe, A Mshl Sir Arthur Coningham (Commander RAF 2nd Tactical Air Force), Lt Gen Lewis Brereton (Commander Allied First Airborne Army) and AVM V.E. Groom. Gen Brereton's US XVIII Airborne Corps was to carry out the airborne crossing of the river; Coningham's 2nd Tactical Air Force provided the overhead cover to the operation. (CL 2223, IWM)

9 March Montgomery issues the final directive for the operation to cross the River Rhine, code name *Plunder*.

10 March The road and rail bridges at Wesel are blown by the retreating Germans as Montgomery's troops reach the Rhine.

21 March A month-long programme of heavy bombing by Allied air forces against German bridges, viaducts and road and rail traffic feeding the Rhine is completed. US Eighth Air Force and the RAF now concentrate their heavy bombers on enemy airfields and barracks to the east of the river.

22 March Gen Patton's US Third Army crosses the Rhine near Nierstein at 2200hrs.

1800hrs The normal harassing fire along the Rhine begins to build in intensity as Allied artillery concentrate on Twenty-First Army Group's sector east of the river prior to the crossings.

2100hrs British Second Army begin Operation *Plunder* with XXX Corps' attacks across the Rhine opposite Rees with 51st (Highland) Division. Heavy opposition from German paratroopers is met once the assaulting battalions move inland.

2200hrs British 1st Commando Brigade cross the Rhine and move to capture the important communications town of Wesel.

2215hrs RAF Bomber Command carry out a heavy bombing raid on Wesel just before 1st Commando Brigade attack the town. The tactical use of these large

The landing site of the 1st Cheshire Regiment located just downstream of Wesel. The viaduct leading to the old railway bridge which once crossed the Rhine is in the right background. The Cheshires crossed over the river to help 1st Commando Brigade clear Wesel during the first morning after the night assault. (Ken Ford)

Naval LCVPs were shipped over to Germany for Operation *Plunder*. The craft went by canal from Antwerp and were then loaded onto tank transporters at Neerharen, before being transferred by road to the Rhine. (BU 2006, IWM)

bombers so close to the attacking troops ensures the success of the operation.

0200hrs British XII Corps attack across the Rhine opposite Xanten with its 15th (Scottish) Division. Enemy resistance is light at first but becomes heavier as the Scottish battalions try to capture the villages inland from the river.

0200hrs US Ninth Army starts its crossing with the 30th Division of XVI Corps attacking over the river south of Wesel. German 180th Division give little opposition to the crossings and swift gains are made.

0300 hours XVI Corps puts its 79th Division across a stretch of the river near Rheinberg, also against negligible opposition.

Daylight Montgomery's forces have established four complete divisions in a bridgehead over the Rhine stretching from Rees to Dinslaken. Enemy opposition starts to increase as more German troops move into the area. German Army Group H Commander, Gen Blaskowitz, releases part of his reserve from XLVII Panzer Corps; 15th Panzergrenadier Division comes south from the Dutch border to counter British XXX Corps' crossings around Rees.

0950hrs The first paratroopers of US XVIII Corps begin their drop in an area to the east of the Diersfordter Forest, north of Wesel. The low-flying transport aircraft and the gliders bringing in the airborne troops, suffer heavy losses from concentrated German anti-aircraft fire. The Diersfordter Forest and the bridges over the River Issel are captured. Contact is later made between the airborne troops and British XII Corps.

2400hrs Montgomery's bridgehead over the Rhine is secure, with only the situation around Rees and the left flank causing any real concern.

25 March More divisions are moving over the Rhine and bridging operations are in progress in all sectors. Enemy artillery fire on the river begins to die down as more and more German batteries are overrun or moved back. Blaskowitz commits more of his reserve and sends 116th Panzer Division against US XVI Corps to the south of the River Lippe. British 15th Division send an armoured column through the airborne landings to engage the enemy on the far side of the bridgehead. American Bailey bridge across the Rhine is opened.

26 March Each of the three infantry corps in the lodgement enlarge their forces with more divisions. As the enemy is pushed back, the extra ground taken is quickly filled by more and more troops.

27 March The German line around the lodgement is starting to break, although resistance is still very strong to the north of Rees on XXX Corps' sector.

28 March Great gains are made as the three infantry corps reach full strength.

29 March The breakout is well under way, with movement out of the bridgehead on all parts of the line. The battle for the Rhine crossings has been won.

Bridging operations on the River Rhine were the most complex of the war. Great stockpiles of Bailey bridging material were assembled prior to the attack. (B 15755, IWM)

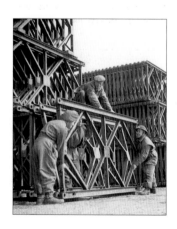

OPPOSING COMMANDERS

The Allied formations opposing the enemy along the Rhine in March 1945 had come a long way since arriving on the mainland of Europe the previous year. The Supreme Commander had brought three army groups into Germany and up to the great river. The Allies had fought many battles and had suffered a few setbacks in their march eastwards. Their armies contained a host of hardened veterans and accomplished commanders, supremely confident in their ability, lavishly supplied with all manner of stores and weapons and all were content in the knowledge that the final victory was in sight. In contrast the Third Reich was collapsing in on itself, shrunk back inside the frontiers of Germany, desperately trying to stem invasion on two fronts, for the Russians were also making great gains in the east. Its commanders were fatalistic, they each knew that the war was lost but that surrender was impossible while a 'madman' was in supreme command. The aggressive generals who had once known nothing but great victories and the conquest of vast tracts of land, were now forced to implement a programme of stopgap defence with inadequate troops and weapons.

ALLIED COMMANDERS

Maj Gen Matthew Ridgway, Commander US XVIII Airborne Corps. Ridgway was one of the most respected of all American commanders with a wealth of experience from his participation in many airborne operations and was much admired by the British. Montgomery preferred that Ridgway's corps with its superior signals systems should control the airborne assault over the Rhine. (US National Archives)

Field Marshal Sir Bernard Montgomery, Commander Twenty-First Army Group, was Britain's most famous and well-loved soldier. Since taking command of the Eighth Army in Egypt, he had accomplished many victories and gained universal admiration. His name was associated with some of the finest feats of arms of the British Army. But all was not as it should be with his Allies. Montgomery's insufferable attitude and almost constant attempts to ensure that his armies ran the show and grabbed the headlines had soured relations with the Americans. Eisenhower regarded Montgomery as a difficult and sometimes prickly subordinate; other American generals thought he was overrated, with a reputation that rested on the overwhelmingly ponderous set-piece battles. To his men, Monty was infallible.

Montgomery's army group contained three armies covering the ground from the North Sea to the junction with Bradley's forces near Düsseldorf: First Canadian Army, Second British Army and US Ninth Army. **Lieutenant-General Henry Crerar** had led the First Canadian Army since it was raised in Normandy. Crerar's army contained a mix of British and Canadian corps and included Polish, Belgian and Dutch formations. It did not perform well in the battles around Falaise and was relegated to clearing out the ports along the Channel coast whilst the remainder of Montgomery's forces dashed towards Germany. Crerar's biggest achievement was Operation *Veritable*, the clearing of the Rhineland. In

15

FM Montgomery, sporting his usual headgear of a black beret, is flanked by American corps and divisional commanders on a visit to Lt Gen Bill Simpson's US Ninth Army's HQ. Front row from left to right: Maj Gen McLain (XIX Corps), Monty, Simpson, Maj Gen Gillem (XIII Corps) and Maj Gen Anderson (XVI Corps)

Lt Gen William Simpson, Commander US Ninth Army. Simpson was a contemporary of Eisenhower at West Point and had seen active service in Mexico and the First World War. (US National Archives)

Lt Gen Sir Neil Ritchie, Commander British XII Corps. Ritchie had seen service in North Africa and had led Eighth Army in Egypt before being relieved of his command by Gen Auchinleck just before First Alamein. Ritchie had commanded XII Corps since Normandy and proved himself an able commander at that level. (B 8222, IWM)

March 1945, after that battle, Crerar's army was located mainly along the Dutch border and was not to be included in the attack across the Rhine, but was intended to supply some of its units for the exploitation of the bridgehead.

Next to the Canadians in the line was British Second Army, the country's most powerful force ever to wage war. It had fought its way from the Normandy beaches into Germany with a string of victories which served to avenge the memory of the British Army's ignominious defeat at Dunkirk in 1940. Second Army was commanded by the mild-mannered **Lieutenant-General Sir Miles Dempsey**, one of Montgomery's protégés who had served with the field marshal in North Africa, Sicily and Italy. Dempsey was a self-effacing, dedicated, professional soldier, immensely loyal to Montgomery and Eisenhower, and equal to the tasks given to him. He totally shunned personal publicity and was still virtually unknown to the public at the end of the war. He was also one of the few senior British commanders who was actually liked by his American equals.

Montgomery's other army commander was the American **Lieutenant General Bill Simpson** who led the US Ninth Army. Simpson was the newcomer to the north-west European theatre, having joined the campaign with Ninth Army in the Autumn of 1944. Tall, bald and amiable, Simpson was a good subordinate to both Montgomery and Bradley. He kept himself clear of all the politics and personalities, being content to fight his army to the best of his ability, no matter whom he reported to. The 57-year-old Simpson had fought with Pershing in Mexico before the First World War and then served with US 33rd Division in France in 1918. The first role given to Simpson's army by Eisenhower was to reduce the fortress city of Brest on the Atlantic coast of France and to contain the German pockets holed up in St Nazaire and Lorient. When he moved his headquarters to the left flank of American forces opposite the Siegfried Line in October 1944, he had units dispersed in five countries: France, Holland, Belgium, Luxembourg and Germany.

Most of Montgomery's corps and divisional commanders had been with him since Normandy. **Lieutenant-General Neil Ritchie**, Commander XII Corps, had at one time commanded Eighth Army in North Africa before Montgomery. Although an able and dedicated commander, Ritchie was not able to bring the leadership to Eighth Army that it needed during its period of retreat. He did, however, later prove himself as a capable corps commander leading XII Corps from Normandy until final victory in Germany. **Lieutenant-General Brian Horrocks**, commander of XXX Corps, was probably Monty's most skilled and likeable corps commander. Like many others, he had been with Montgomery in North Africa and would have served in Italy as well if he had not been badly wounded in Tunisia. Horrocks was an amiable individual, liked by the Americans and loved by those who served under him.

US VI Corps would make Ninth Army's assault, under the command of **Major General John Anderson.** Anderson's corps had entered the front line for the first time only the previous month when it took over a holding position on the left flank of Ninth Army's Grenade offensive. The attack across the Rhine was to be Anderson's first battle as corps commander. In contrast to the newly raised VI Corps' HQ, Anderson's two assault divisions were veteran outfits with experienced commanders. **Major General Ira Wyche** had fought his 79th Division from the Normandy battlefields through France to the German borders. **Major General Leland Hobbs** had likewise been in many battles with his 30th Division since early June.

Lt Gen Sir Brian Horrocks, Commander XXX Corps. Horrocks was one of Montgomery's favourite generals, having been with the field marshal in the desert with Eighth Army and was badly injured in Tunisia. In late July Horrocks took command of XXX Corps in Normandy and led the corps for the remainder of the war through some of the fiercest battles fought by Second Army. (B9301, IWM)

GenFM Albert Kesselring German Commander-in-Chief (West). Kesselring was a Luftwaffe general who had gained a well deserved reputation as a commander of both air and ground troops. His masterful defence of Italy against two Allied armies, prompted Hitler to decide to bring him north to organize the defence of Germany. Able though he was, Kesselring's appointment was too late for him to have any material effect on the eventual outcome. (NARA, Washington).

GERMAN COMMANDERS

Generalfeldmarschall Gerd von Rundstedt had been Commander-in-Chief West during the Normandy campaign, but was relieved of his command when he suggested a planned withdrawal from the region to a new line behind the River Seine. Hitler, however, realized that the old field marshal was still one of his most able generals and reinstated him to his old command prior to the Ardennes offensive in December. Von Rundstedt was, however, a realist and when the attack was finally abandoned in January 1945 he knew that Germany was heading for certain defeat. The loss of the bridge over the Rhine at Remagen on 7 March 1945 proved to be his downfall. Hitler once again lost confidence in the field marshal and replaced him with the more charismatic and energetic GenFM Kesselring, whose skilful defence of Italy had singled him out as one of Germany's most able generals.

Generalfeldmarschall Albert Kesselring had been a Luftwaffe officer since joining the newly raised service in 1933. It was as an air-general that he rose to high command, leading *Luftflotte 1* in the Polish campaign and *Luftflotte 2* during the Battle of Britain. He then saw service in Russia before taking command of all German air and land troops in the Mediterranean. It was no easy task, for the early successes of Rommel and his Afrika Korps in North Africa soon gave way to a never-ending series of setbacks and withdrawals, as German and Italian formations found it difficult to contain the ever stronger Allied armies sent to the region. After the Axis collapse in Tunisia, Sicily and then Italy became targets for Eisenhower's next moves. What should have been a

General der Panzertruppen Heinrich Freiherr von Lüttwitz, Commander German XLVII Panzer Corps. The aristocratic Von Lüttwitz had commanded 2nd and 20th Panzer Divisions in Russia and took command of XLVII Panzer Corps in September 1944. He later directed the besieging forces at Bastogne during Hitler's Ardennes offensive. In March 1945, at the time of the Rhine crossings, LXVII Panzer Corps was German Army Group H's only reserve. (US National Archives)

disaster for the Germans became something of a triumph when Kesselring set about a masterly defence of the long Italian peninsula, making the Allies fight for every metre of land. Two Allied armies were tied up in the Italian theatre for almost two years, struggling to gain advantage over Kesselring's sparse forces.

On 10 March 1945, GenFM Kesselring took over the front which extended from the Dutch coast on the North Sea down to the Alps. In the north, opposite Montgomery's forces, was German Army Group H. In the centre, opposing Gen Bradley's Twelfth Army Group was German Army Group B. In the south, opposite Gen Dever's Sixth Army Group, was German Army Group G.

Commanding Army Group H was one of the most senior of the German generals, **Generaloberst Johannes Blaskowitz**. An infantryman of the old school, he was born in 1878 and gradually rose through the officer class to reach the rank of Generalleutnant in 1935. In 1939 he was promoted to Gen der Infanterie and given command of Heeresgruppe II at Dresden just before the war. He later led German Eighth Army in the attack on Poland and was present at the Polish surrender. His reward was the position as Commander-in-Chief of the Army of Occupation. Then things went wrong for Blaskowitz. He became appalled at the conduct of the SS in Poland and sent a note about their behaviour to GenFM Brauchitsch. Hitler got to hear of it and the incident blighted Blaskowitz's career. He was omitted from the grand promotions of 1940 when many generals junior to him were elevated to field marshal. He was not given another fighting command for the next four years until after the Allied invasion of Normandy. Blaskowitz had two armies under his command: Twenty-Fifth Army in Holland and First Parachute Army along the northern Rhine opposite Montgomery.

The commander of German First Parachute Army was a Luftwaffe general with an outstanding fighting record. **Gen der Fallschirmtruppen Alfred Schlemm** had a reputation for being a resolute defensive commander gained by his masterly handling of I Parachute Corps in Italy, most notably in the containment of the Anzio beachhead. He had come to Italy after service in Crete, as Gen Student's Chief of Staff, and Russia where his actions at Smolensk and Vitebsk earned him great praise. Seen by Kesselring as 'impulsive and brilliant', Schlemm was obliged to continue to fight his formations defensively against the inexorable advances of the Allies. In the Rhineland offensive, his First Parachute Army had resisted Canadian First Army with all the power he could muster, making Gen Crerar's army fight a long bitter battle to gain the west bank of the Rhine, whilst all the while trying to delay US Ninth Army coming up from the south. Schlemm maintained an unbroken front until the last moment, when his army had to make a fighting withdrawal to avoid encirclement. He was ordered by Hitler not to allow any bridge over the Rhine to fall into enemy hands, on penalty of death. As he later remarked: 'Since I had nine bridges in my army sector, I could see my hopes for a long life rapidly dwindling.'

Commanding II Parachute Corps was another *Luftwaffe* general, Eugen Meindl. **General der Fallschirmtruppen Meindl** had transferred to airborne forces from the army in 1940. He led an assault regiment in the Maleme sector during the invasion of Crete and then commanded a division in Russia. In late 1943, Meindl was given the newly formed II

Parachute Corps in Eastern France. After the invasion of Normandy, Meindl's corps was given the task of trying to contain the US VII and IXX Corps and later took part in the battles for St Lo and the American break-out. The II Parachute Corps was virtually destroyed in the Falaise encirclement but later regrouped under First Parachute Army for the defence of Germany.

Schlemm's other corps holding the river line was LXXXVI Corps, under the command of **General der Infanterie Erich Straube**. Gen Straube had commanded LXXIV Corps in the Heurtgen Forest battles against the Americans in November 1944. His command was a very weak one, consisting of just the 89th and 347th Divisions, both of which had been savaged during the closing of the Falaise gap in Normandy. They were reconstructed from various miscellaneous units and sent back into the line defending the West Wall defences. So under-strength was the 347th Division, that when a training battalion, a fortress battalion and a 'stomach' battalion were attached, the newcomers exceeded the original personnel by more than ten to one. Not surprisingly, Straube's corps performed badly and he was relieved of his command in early 1945 and given a new role of guarding the east bank of the Rhine with LXXXVI Corps.

Gen Blaskowitz's army reserve was XLVII Panzer Corps, commanded by a general with a sound reputation from Russia, **General der Panzertruppen Heinrich Freiherr von Lüttwitz**. The 59-year-old Von Lüttwitz had led both the 2nd and 20th Panzer Divisions in Russia and was later given command of XLVII Panzer Corps in the west in September 1944. During the Ardennes offensive, his corps was one of the lead formations of Gen Manteuffel's Fifth Panzer Army and laid the siege to the important town of Bastogne.

GenObst Johannes Blaskowitz, Commander German Army Group H, one of the most senior of all German generals. He commanded the Eighth Army in the campaign in Poland in 1939, afterwards becoming head of the occupation troops there. His outspoken views on the atrocities committed by the SS led to him being passed over for promotion to field marshal. Blaskowitz had to wait four long years until he was given another field command. (PL 83971, IWM)

OPPOSING FORCES

When Gen Eisenhower brought his Allied armies up to the Rhine in March 1945 to face those of GenFM Kesselring, he did so from a position of force. Eighty-five American, British, Canadian, French and Polish divisions lined up against 55 German divisions. Most of these Allied divisions were well up to strength, although by no means all of them had their full complement of men. In contrast, all of Kesselring's formations were well below their normal strength. In his autobiography, the German field marshal claimed that the daily strength of each of his infantry divisions at that time was on average only 5,000 men, against an establishment of 12,000. In fact, many of them were much worse off than that. Kesselring lamented that he had only 100 combatants available for each kilometre of front. Against this sparse defence in the sector of the northern Rhine, Montgomery was planning to unleash three armies containing 29 divisions with more than a million and a quarter men.

ALLIED FORCES

In the operations to clear the Rhineland in February and March 1945 – operations *Veritable* and *Grenade* – Montgomery's forces had conducted what was the last stand-up fight in the west. This final battle of attrition had cleared the way to the River Rhine and swept aside most of the strength that the enemy had facing the western Allies. From here on in, to the end of the war, the fighting could only be a one-sided affair. The

American light Chaffee tanks disembark from US naval landing craft after crossing the Rhine. US Navy LCVP Unit No 3 provided 24 LCVP (Landing Craft Vehicle and Personnel) and 24 LCM (Landing Craft Medium) for Ninth Army's support and supply missions. (KY 488962, IWM)

Scottish infantry of the Highland Division have their first meal on the far side of the River Rhine on the morning after the night attack. (BU 2159, IWM)

might of western industrial production and training was pitted against a worn-out force incapable of rejuvenation. In the east, the inexorable Russian juggernaut ground down all German resistance in front of it.

British Second Army had landed in Normandy on 6 June 1944 and had taken part in all of the fighting in Normandy and the advance into Germany. It was the prime British formation in north-west Europe, Montgomery's main strike force. To its corps and divisions were sent the best of all that was available in Britain. It carried with it the prestige of the British Army and Montgomery always manoeuvred to have it involved in what he saw as the main Allied attacks.

Canadian First Army had become operational in Normandy at the end of July. It made slow progress in the drive to seize Falaise and to form the northern part of a great manoeuvre to encircle the trapped German Seventh and Fifth Panzer Armies. Montgomery was not impressed and for the next six months gave Canadian First Army the role of securing the left flanks of British Second Army's advance. This changed in January 1945 when Crerar was given the task of commanding the last great stand-up fight with the Germans in the Rhineland battle. For the Rhine crossing, Crerar's army again had the task of acting as flank guard.

Gen Bill Simpson's Ninth Army began its operational life on 5 September 1944 when it took command of all US forces in the Brittany Peninsula. At that time the war had moved eastwards and Simpson's role was to reduce those German forces holed up in the fortresses that surrounded the Brittany ports of Brest, Lorient and St Nazaire. After a long siege, already twelve days old when Ninth Army assumed command, and a very bitter struggle costing almost 3,000 casualties, Brest was finally taken on 18 September. The great port proved to be useless to the Allies

The first German prisoners are brought back to the river through 15th (Scottish) Division's lines ready to be transported across to the Allied shore in the Buffalo LVTs of 79th Armoured Division. (BU 2107, IWM)

for all of its installations had been shattered and destroyed. So fanatical was the German resistance, and so complete was the destruction, that Eisenhower decided that it was not worth the effort to try to capture the remaining ports. Lorient and St Nazaire were surrounded and the enemy inside were left bottled up until the end of the war.

After Brittany, US Ninth Army was moved into the line on the German border between British Second Army and US First Army. In February 1945 under the command of British 21st Army Group it took part in the Rhineland battle, launching Operation *Grenade* to clear the enemy from the area between the Dutch border and the River Rhine. It remained under Montgomery's command for the Rhine crossings.

FM Montgomery's million and a quarter men waiting to cross the Rhine were about to carry out an amphibious assault that rivalled the Normandy invasion, not only in the number of troops involved, but in the scale of the support operation. Prodigious amounts of supplies, transport and special equipment were involved; the complexity and scale of the airborne support approached that of D-Day. The British assembled 60,000 tons of ammunition and 30,000 tons of engineering stores as well as a further 26,000 tons of other stores. All this was in addition to the normal daily usage rates. The US Ninth Army built up 138,000 tons of supplies and amassed 2,070 pieces of ordnance, while the British and Canadians assembled 3,411 artillery pieces, anti-tank and anti-aircraft guns and rocket launchers.

ALLIED ORDER OF BATTLE

Twenty-First Army Group *Field Marshal Sir Bernard Montgomery*

British Second Army *Lt Gen Sir Miles Dempsey*

Assault Formations

GHQ 4th Independent Armoured Brigade *Brig R.M.P. Carver*
    31st Armoured Brigade (From 79th Armoured Division) *Brig G.S. Knight*
    33rd Armoured Brigade (From 79th Armoured Division) *Brig H.B. Scott*
XII Corps *Lt Gen Sir Neil Ritchie*
    7th Armoured Division *Maj Gen L.O. Lyne*
    15th (Scottish) Division *Maj Gen C.M. Barber*
    52nd (Lowland) Division *Maj Gen E. Hakewill Smith*
    53rd (Welsh) Division *Maj Gen R.K. Ross*
    1st Commando Brigade *Brig D. Mills Roberts*
    115th Infantry Brigade (attached) *Brig E.L. Luce*

XXX Corps *Lt Gen Sir Brian Horrocks*
    Guards Armoured Division *Maj Gen Alan Adair*
    3rd Division *Maj Gen L.G. Whistler*
    43rd (Wessex) Division *Maj Gen G. Ivor Thomas*
    51st (Highland) Division *Maj Gen T.G. Rennie later Maj Gen MacMillan*
    Canadian 9th Infantry Brigade (attached) *Brig J.M. Rockingham*
    Canadian 3rd Division *Maj Gen Dan Spry*
    8th Armoured Brigade *Brig Prior Palmer*

US XVIII Airborne Corps *Maj Gen Matthew Ridgway*
    British 6th Airborne Division *Maj Gen Eric Bols*
    US 17th Airborne Division *Maj Gen William Miley*

Follow-up Formations

Canadian II Corps *Lt Gen Guy Simmonds*
Canadian 4th Armoured Division *Maj Gen C. Vokes*
Canadian 2nd Division *Maj Gen A.B. Matthews*

Reserve Formations

VIII Corps *Lt Gen E.H. Barker*
11th Armoured Division *Maj Gen 'Pip' Roberts*
6th Guards Armoured Brigade *Brig W.D.C. Greenacre*

US Ninth Army

Assault Formation

XVI Corps *Maj Gen John Anderson*
8th Armored Division *Brig Gen John Devine*
30th Division *Maj Gen Leland Hobbs*
35th Division *Maj Gen Paul Baade*
75th Division *Maj Gen Ray Porter*
79th Division *Maj Gen Ira Wyche*

Follow Up Formations

XIX Corps *Maj Gen Raymond McLain*
2nd Armored Division *Brig Gen I.D. White*
29th Division *Maj Gen Charles Gerhardt*
83rd Division *Maj Gen Robert Macon*
95th Division *Maj Gen Harry Twaddle*

XIII Corps *Maj Gen Alvan Gillen*
5th Armored Division *Maj Gen Lunsford Oliver*
84th Division *Maj Gen Alexander Bolling*
102nd Division *Maj Gen Frank Keating*

GERMAN FORCES

While Montgomery gathered his irresistible armies west of the Rhine, his opposite number on the German side of the river was trying to bring together some semblance of a force to resist him. The strongest of Blaskowitz's two armies, Schlemm's First Parachute Army, was given the sector along which an Allied attack was expected – between Emmerich and Dinslaken – with Gen d.Inf von Blumentritt's Twenty-Fifth Army ordered to hold the river downstream from Emmerich to the North Sea. Neither of these two formations was anywhere near its nominal strength; both had been badly mauled in the winter fighting west of the Rhine.

Morale amongst the Germans was low as they waited for the imminent attack across the river. As GenMaj Karl Wagener, Chief of Staff of Army Group B, later explained, 'It varied from suspicion to callous resignation. The army could only pretend to resist.' The question on everyone's minds was, where and when would the crossing take place? All they could do was to set about preparing the lower reaches ready for the onslaught with an air of resignation, knowing that the war was in all probability lost. Resistance continued because no one had the courage to persuade the madman who led the nation that it was time to stop.

Troops of 53rd (Welsh) Division advance eastwards from the Rhine bridgehead in the relative security of a Kangaroo armoured personnel carrier provided by 79th Armoured Division. The carriers were modified Canadian-built RAM tanks with turrets and associated equipment removed, allowing 11 fully laden troops to be carried. It had a crew of two men. (BU 2956, IWM)

By the end of March 1945 German troop strength was haemorrhaging at a rate that was unsustainable. Every man under 45 able to take up arms had already been press-ganged into the *Volkssturm*. Few replacements were available to make up the losses suffered in the previous months, so each division had to carry on with the men it had. The whole of Gen d.Fallschirm Meindl's II Parachute Corps, the strongest enemy formation opposing British Second Army, contained only 12,000 men, well below the strength of just one Allied Division.

The II Parachute Corps comprised three parachute divisions who had already seen a good deal of action against the Allies on the Western Front. All of them, however, had been in existence for just a relatively short time. The most senior of the three, the 6th Parachute Division, had been raised in Amiens in June 1944 and was immediately fed into the fighting in Normandy against the Allied landings. By September, when fighting in the battle of the Mons Pocket, it had a combat strength of just two battalions. Reorganized and reinforced it then had the misfortune of having to immediately oppose the Arnhem operation, the battle for Holland and the Canadian-led Rhineland offensive.

The 7th Parachute Regiment had been hastily created as Parachute Division Erdmann in September 1944 and sent against the British corridor that led to Arnhem. It successfully helped to delay the relief of British 1st Parachute Division landings, which in turn allowed II SS-Panzer Corps to annihilate this first Allied bridgehead over the Rhine. After the battle this emergency parachute formation was fully upgraded to the 7th Parachute Division and reinforced with elite personnel from parachute and Waffen-SS schools, as well as combat groups from the 6th Parachute Division. As part of II Parachute Corps, it fought and was depleted in the Rhineland battle.

The last, and most recent, of the parachute divisions in the corps was 8th Parachute Division. It had been raised in the Cologne area three months previously, in December 1944. Falling numbers of trained German personnel meant that it never had enough troops to form a full division and it never exceeded regimental strength. What little power it did have was further reduced during the Rhineland battle.

The latest British tank to enter the fighting in north-west Europe was the Comet, which arrived in small quantities in late December 1944. Here a Comet of 11th Armoured Division joins in the drive across Germany from out of the bridgehead. The tank was an improved version of the Cromwell armed with a shorter 17-pdr gun (77mm) and was probably the best British tank of the war, but its arrival in battle was a little too late. (BU 2760, IWM)

Facing the right wing of British Second and US Ninth Army's crossing places was the German LXXXVI Corps, commanded by Gen d.Inf Erich Straube. Its 84th Division held the river below Wesel and its 180th Division was along the Rhine upstream of the town. The 84th Division had been formed in Poland early in 1944 then sent to the fighting in Normandy after the D-Day landings. It was almost annihilated in the Falaise pocket in August 1944, with just one regiment able to escape the debacle. Re-formed in September, it later joined II Parachute Corps for the Arnhem and Rhineland battles. The 180th Division was formed as a replacement and training division in 1939 and spent most of the war carrying out that role in northern Germany. In September 1944, at the time of the German collapse in the west, it was sent to Holland to help stem the Allied advance. Two months later it was upgraded to full infantry division status.

Upstream of LXXXVI Corps was Gen d.Inf Erich Abraham's LXIII Corps. It covered a sector that was thought less likely to be the main Allied crossing place and was a corps in name only, containing just one regular formation, the 2nd Parachute Division, and a scratch force optimistically labelled the 'Hamburg' Division of which little is known save that it consisted of a collection of troops from various disciplines, all hastily armed and sent into the line.

It was not just poor troop numbers that hampered the Germans in their defence of the Rhine, for weapons and equipment were equally as sparse. In all of Army Group H's reserve, there were only 35 tanks; the whole of the army group itself contained just 200 tanks and assault guns. It did, however, have on call a reasonable complement of artillery, including a *Volks* artillery corps and a *Volkswerfer* brigade. This firepower reserve was further increased by the withdrawal of almost all mobile anti-aircraft units from Holland. These were placed in positions to assist the 81 heavy and 252 light anti-aircraft pieces in batteries along the Rhine, concentrated for the most part around Wesel, the area already located by the enemy as the most likely site for airborne landings.

GenFM Kesselring inspected the arrangements to resist the Rhine crossings on 14 March and gave his approval. Despite this he had little expectation that his preparations could successfully hold a determined assault across the river. Should a foothold be gained by Montgomery, Kesselring had no other reserves to send to Army Group H's assistance.

GERMAN ORDER OF BATTLE

C-in-C West *GenFM Albert Kesselring*

Army Group H *GenObst Johannes Blaskowitz*

Army Group Reserve
    XLVII Panzer Corps *Gen d.PzTp Heinrich von Lüttwitz*
        15th Panzer Grenadier *GenMaj Wolfgang Maucke*
        116th Panzer Division *GenMaj Siegfried von Waldenburg*
  First Parachute Army *Gen d.Fallschirm Alfred Schlemm*
  II Parachute Corps *Gen d.Fallschirm Eugen Meindl*
      6th Parachute Division *GenLt Hermannn Plocher*
      7th Parachute Division *GenLt Wolfgang Erdmann*
      8th Parachute Division *GenLt Wadehn*

    LXXXVI Corps *Gen d.Inf Erich Straube*
      84th Division *Oberst Siegfried Kossack*
      180th Division *GenMaj Bernhard Klosterkemper*

    LXIII Corps *Gen der Inf Erich Abraham*
      Division Hamburg
      2nd Parachute Division *GenLt Walther Lackner*

Committed later against the crossings

To XLVII Panzer Corps
      190th Division *Lt Gen Ernst Hammer*

OPPOSING PLANS

Planning for the Rhine crossing began in November 1944, just two months after the failure of Montgomery's Operation *Market Garden*. The September attack had been an ambitious one, completely out of character for this normally cautious general. He had planned to seize bridges over the Maas, the Waal and then the lower Rhine at Arnhem, using a combination of airborne and ground troops. Montgomery intended to lay an airborne carpet from the inside of the Belgian border into Holland and then roll up the enemy resistance on the far side of the Rhine with ground troops. (See Campaign 24: *Arnhem Campaign 1944*). The attack was the largest airborne assault of the war and ended in catastrophic failure and much recrimination. Not unexpectedly, the Allied generals learned a good many lessons from the debacle. Montgomery was determined that the same mistakes would not be made again when the time came for another attempt to cross the Rhine. He intended that the river would be taken by a massive set-piece operation the scale of which would almost match the D-Day invasion of Normandy.

A British Achilles self-propelled gun armed with a 17-pdr weapon crosses the main glider landing ground, LZ P, east of Hamminkeln. (BU 2396, IWM)

ALLIED PLANS

FM Montgomery's final directive for the operation to cross the River Rhine, code name *Plunder*, was issued on 9 March 1945. Its objective was quite straightforward: 'to cross the Rhine north of the Ruhr and secure a firm bridgehead, with a view to developing operations to isolate the Ruhr and to penetrate deeper into Germany.' The area chosen for the assault was between Emmerich and Rheinburg, with the flat area inland between Rees and Wesel the most likely location for an airborne landing.

In outline, Montgomery's original plan called for the Rhine to be crossed by British Second Army with a single two-division corps from US Ninth Army under command. US Ninth Army would not participate in the assault, but would join the operation during the breakout phase. Not surprisingly, Lt Gen Bill Simpson was 'flabbergasted'. It seemed inconceivable that his army would not be used in the attack phase of the operation and that only two of his American divisions would participate in the greatest river assault of the war. Lt Gen Dempsey, Commander British Second Army, was equally amazed at this affront to American prestige and to the logistical complications that would arise in trying to pass the whole of Ninth Army through his bridgehead. Dempsey joined Simpson in criticism of Montgomery's plans and they submitted a revised plan of their own for consideration. This included a fuller American involvement in the assault and a much wider area of attack to include Canadian First Army. Montgomery saw them halfway, agreeing to an American attack by Ninth Army south of Wesel, but declined to include the Canadian army in his assault, although he did agree to a Canadian brigade being attached to 51st Division. Canadian First Army would follow the assault phase with part of its force and then begin operations down the Rhine into Holland.

The actual crossing places for the revised attack would be located between Rees and Rheinburg where the slow Rhine had over the centuries carved out a flat plain some ten to 15 kilometres wide. Along this section of river the Rhine was bordered with modern high dykes or bunds, reinforced against flooding. Central to the plan was the

Troops of 154th Brigade, from 51st (Highland) Division, board stormboats ready for their swift journey across the Rhine early in the morning of 24 March. The men are most likely from the 1st Black Watch, the brigade's third battalion, who were following up the previous night's assault crossings. (BU 2167, IWM)

A paratrooper from US XVIII Airborne Corps welcomes a British tanker into the American bridgehead with a cigarette. (BU 2738, IWM)

immediate capture of Wesel with its communications centre, sited almost in the middle of the assault area.

Once the British lodgement had been established, expansion of the bridgehead was to progress in three directions: southwards to secure the road network around Wesel from enemy ground attack, northwards to seize Emmerich, its road centre and new bridging sites, and eastwards to establish a firm base from which further offensive operations into Germany could be developed. In the south, Simpson's army was to do likewise, advancing northwards to meet the British at Wesel, southwards to protect the flank facing the Rhur industrial area and eastwards to carve out room for the follow-up divisions to manoeuvre.

The opening assault was to be made by two corps from British Second Army and by the single corps of US Ninth Army. The attacks were to be given the maximum support of Allied strategic and tactical air forces, together with the largest artillery concentrations possible. Shortly after the river assaults had been made, they would be followed by a corps of airborne troops landing on the far side of the river just ahead of the ground troops. Montgomery planned to have large parts of three armies east of the Rhine and north of the Ruhr ready to deploy in any direction that might be ordered by the Supreme Commander within three days.

Lt Gen Dempsey selected XXX and XII Corps from his Second Army to make the British assault. XXX Corps would begin the attack at 2100hrs on 23 March, crossing the river in the Rees sector. An hour later, 1st Commando Brigade was to cross three kilometres downstream of Wesel and then advance up the river to capture the town. At 0200hrs the next morning, XII Corps would attack opposite Xanten. At the same time, US Ninth Army would begin its assault from a site farther upstream to the north of Rheinberg with a crossing by US XVI Corps.

To help protect the inland side of the lodgement area from enemy attack and to clear the area overlooking the river, US XVIII Airborne Corps was to be dropped a few kilometres east of the Rhine. Its two airborne divisions were to land and establish a bridgehead eight to 15 kilometres long and eight kilometres deep. The designated landing and drop zones for the corps were to be located close enough to the Rhine to be supported by Allied artillery immediately after their arrival and close enough also to allow both ground and airborne troops to link up on the first day of the operation. To help expedite an expansion to the east, key bridges over the River Issel which ran across the proposed line of advance would also be seized The airborne attack would go in on the morning after the night river assault. The decision to use these elite troops so near to the crossing places in daylight came in for criticism both before and after the event. It was suggested that they were too close to the river assault to have a material effect on the outcome of the attack and that they would be more vulnerable to enemy flak than if they came in at night.

GERMAN PLANS

The Germans knew that an attack across the River Rhine in the north was inevitable and could only make hasty arrangements for a defence of the river to repel it. Their final strategy was based on three main elements, the first of which was the river itself. The Rhine had few fixed defences on which to mount a resistance, for Hitler had relied on the Siegfried Line as his main stop line and this had already been totally breached by the Allies. The Germans hoped that the swift current and wide expanse of the river would help slow down and defeat an attack. Failing that, the next element in their plan was to rely on the troops based along the east bank of the river. These infantry would attempt to kill any assault whilst it was actually on the Rhine itself with machine-gun, mortar and artillery fire and then seal any lodgement that was established ashore as it formed, ready for later annihilation. They had hastily built a series of field fortifications along the forward line of the river, together with a rear line based along the railways and an unfinished autobahn that ran parallel to the Rhine. Both Rees and Wesel had anti-tank ditches to the north of the towns, but there was little time to create positions of any depth anywhere along the far side of the river.

The third part of the strategy was based on mobility. Should the Allies establish a bridgehead and start to move inland, then armoured units would move against them and sweep them back into the river. This was wishful thinking, for the only armoured formations in a position to oppose Montgomery were the few tanks left in the two depleted divisions that made up Army Group H's only reserve, the XLVII Panzer Corps. Such a plan might have been effective if Gen Blaskowitz had earlier been able to preserve intact a sizeable number of the formations in Army Group H, but Hitler's 'no retreat' philosophy meant that most of his strength had been squandered west of the river. The scratch forces

German war cemetery at Diersfordt, just inside the forest near the castle, containing 385 burials of the men caught up in the first two days of the Rhine assault. (Ken Ford)

assembled on the Rhine to resist Montgomery were divisions in name only. Most had so few troops available that they barely had enough men to form a single regiment.

Kesselring knew that the area around Wesel was the most logical place for Montgomery to cross and had massed around ten of his best divisions with 30 kilometres of the expected assault area. Holding the sector opposite Twenty-First Army Group was Gen der Fallschirmtruppen Alfred Schlemm's German First Parachute Army. Along the river line between Emmerich and Dinslaken were two German corps: II Parachute and LXXXVI Corps, with the armoured formations of XLVII Panzer Corps in the rear near the Dutch–German border.

The II Parachute Corps had three divisions in the line in front of Montgomery: 6th Parachute Division north-west of Rees, 8th Parachute Division around Rees and 7th Parachute Division south of Rees. Straube's LXXXVI Corps held the river on the left of II Parachute Corps with 84th Division either side of Wesel and 180th Division along the river south of Wesel to the area of Dinslaken. Straube also had garrison troops in Wesel made up from various local *Volkssturm* troops, Luftwaffe personnel and local security units. The mobile formations of Von Lüttwitz's XLVII Panzer Corps east of the Rhine contained just the remnants of the 15th Panzer Grenadier Division and the 116th Panzer Division.

Kesselring and Blaskowitz both knew that the area to the north of Wesel and to the east of the Diersfordter Forest was the most likely place for any airborne assault. A few tanks were therefore put into the forest to defend the artillery batteries emplaced there, with orders to move against any airborne landings should they take place. Also placed in depth around this area were many Luftwaffe anti-aircraft batteries, capable of being used in a dual role against both aircraft and land troops.

31

THE BRITISH ASSAULT

Lt Gen Sir Miles Dempsey planned to make Second Army's assault across the Rhine with two corps: XXX Corps (Lt Gen Brian Horrocks) on the left and XII Corps (Lt Gen Neil Ritchie) on the right. The honour of making these initial attacks would go to two Scottish divisions: the 51st (Highland) Division (Maj Gen Rennie) of XXX Corps would make landfall either side of the small town of Rees and the 15th (Scottish) Division (Maj Gen Barber) from XII Corps would cross to the area opposite Xanten. Joining in this initial assault was 1st Commando Brigade (Brig Mills Roberts) which would cross just downstream of Wesel and then advance inland to take the town from the rear. Its task was to seize Wesel and hold its important road junctions until relieved by troops from US 17th Parachute Division (Maj Gen Miley) who were to land mid-morning the next day. The crossings would begin on the night of 23 March 1945, with H-hour for the first assault at 2200hrs.

51st (HIGHLAND) DIVISION

Right on time, at 2100hrs, 51st (Highland) Division's assault crossing of the River Rhine, Operation *Turnscrew*, took to the water, its way prepared by a tremendous artillery barrage that had been pounding the far shore since 1800hrs. Beneath the roar of hundreds of shells passing low overhead, the first of the Buffaloes carrying the troops of 154th Brigade's two lead battalions moved out across the river. The crossing took just two-and-a-half minutes. Little enemy opposition was encountered on the river and, just six minutes after the start of the operation, the commanding officers of both 7th Argyll and Sutherland Highlanders and the 7th Black Watch were able to report back to brigade HQ that their battalions had landed on the other side of the river.

As the Scottish battalions moved ashore there were some casualties from anti-personnel mines. One Buffalo carrying men of the 7th Black Watch was blown up by a Teller mine. Enemy resistance along the river line was slight, but as the Scotsmen moved inland this opposition became more intense. Resistance nests had been established among the small hamlets and groups of houses which overlooked the river. These strongpoints slowed up the expansion of the beachhead, but none of them were strong enough to do more than introduce a slight delay to the plans of the two assault battalions. Those of the enemy holding the line of the Rhine were mainly from German 8th Parachute Division, the bulk of which was more firmly established in solid defensive positions amongst the hamlets and villages back from the river.

On the left of the landings, 7th Black Watch took all of its objectives and anchored the northern flank of the crossings around Wardmannshof

Troops of 15th (Scottish) Division cross the River Rhine in stormboats in daylight on the morning of 24 March. (BU 2155, IWM)

and Scholtenhof. On the right, 7th Argylls had touched down exactly where planned and seized Ratshoff and the road crossings east of Rees. At 2230hrs, the third battalion of 154th Brigade crossed over and passed through the Argylls to take up the advance inland. The 1st Black Watch attacked Kleinesserden and the enemy strongpoint located just north of the village, meeting the fiercest enemy resistance encountered thus far in the operation. It took the battalion almost the whole of the night to subdue these objectives and to advance on to the next village of Speldrop. By dawn 1st Black Watch reported to Brigade HQ that both villages were free of the enemy.

The other of the Highland Division's lead brigades that night was 153rd Brigade. It also planned to carry out a two-battalion assault across the Rhine, with landings either side of Rees. The 5th Black Watch crossed on the left, landing downstream of Rees without difficulty establishing a secure bridgehead and then moving inland to attack Esserden. Fighting for possession of the village carried on throughout the night and it was not until first light that the objective was finally taken. On the right, upstream of Rees, the 5th/7th Gordon Highlanders crossed against light opposition and was soon able to secure a safe lodgement. Its location, however, was at something of a disadvantage as it was separated from Rees by a strip of backwater named the Alter Rhine. During the night the Gordons were able to eliminate all enemy presence from this 'island', but were unable to get onto the mainland close by Rees. As darkness gave way to light, enemy snipers dominated this small beachhead and made all movement in the open difficult. The battalion remained pinned down, unable to move for the rest of the day.

The third of 153rd Brigade's battalions, the 1st Gordon Highlanders, followed the 5th Black Watch over the river just as soon as the returning Buffaloes were able to carry its troops across. The Gordons were ferried over the Rhine without a single casualty. They passed through the Black Watch and by morning had penetrated inland across the Rees–Speldrop road. The two lead companies then swung right to attack the western outskirts of Rees. A few hours later the battalion had three companies methodically clearing their way through the town, moving inexorably towards the strongpoint situated in the ruins of the town's large church.

The Gordons were assisted in their clearing of the town by a gun-crew from 454th Mountain Battery RA, led by Capt McNair. The battery was equipped with archaic 3.7in howitzers which could be broken down into pieces for ease of transport. This type of gun was often seen at military tattoos, raced over obstacles by their crews for entertainment. The 454th Mountain Battery had been training in Scotland for three years and had been specially selected for the Rhine crossings. Each gun was carried over the river in a Buffalo, landing with the leading troops. Capt McNair managed to move his guns right into Rees and was able to

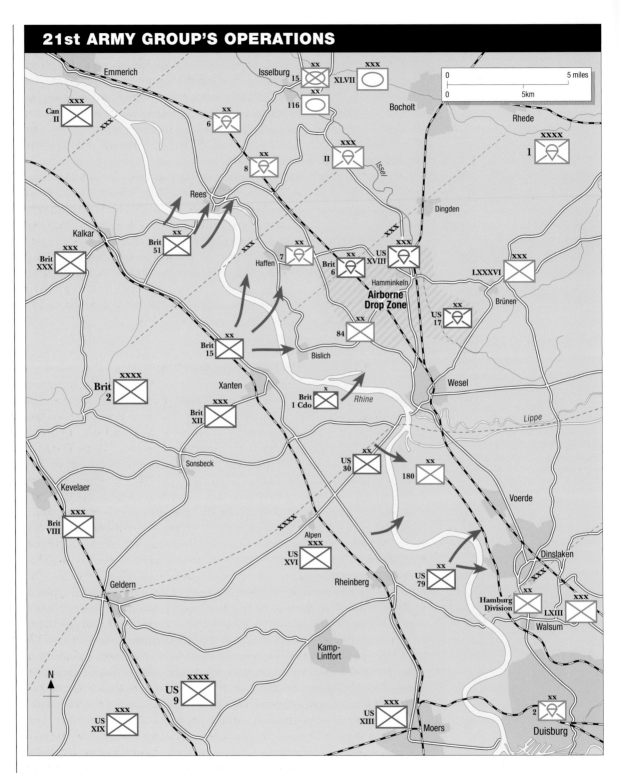

support the Gordons at almost point blank range. His gun crews hauled them over rubble, round corners and through houses, bringing devastating fire down on the heads of the opposition as directed by the Scotsmen. On one occasion Capt McNair's men actually took a gun to bits and mounted it in an upstairs room.

Maj Gen Rennie began introducing the third of his formations over the Rhine just before midnight, when 152nd Brigade's lead battalion, 2nd Seaforth Highlanders, crossed in stormboats to join 5th Black Watch. The battalion moved northwards to the far end of Rees and was involved in much heavy fighting around the factory area, trying to establish a position from which an attack could be put in against the village of Mittelburg. The 5th Queen's Own Camerons came up to join the Seaforths, but further progress across an anti-tank ditch which barred their way proved impossible.

The 152nd Brigade's third battalion, the 5th Seaforth, had been held back in reserve and finally crossed the river at dawn on the 24th. During the night many stormboats had been knocked out or had broken down and the 5th Seaforth's passage across the Rhine was slow, only completed piecemeal in small groups. The battalion then moved to a forming-up area south of Esserden where it was subjected to almost constant shelling. It was later sent northwards to the factory area and became mixed up with the Camerons trying to put in their attack on Mittelburg. The battalion waited all day to go into action. Eventually it was ordered to capture the small village of Groin to the east of Mittelburg.

1st COMMANDO BRIGADE

At the same time that 51st Division was launching its attack across the River Rhine in the north of British Second Army's sector, the leading troops of 1st Commando Brigade had moved to their forming-up places ready to begin Operation *Widgeon*, the attack to capture Wesel. The men of 46 Royal Marine Commando were in Ginderich on board the Buffaloes which were to carry them over the Rhine, while those of 6 Commando moved through the darkness to a backwater 2,000 metres downstream of the intended crossing places. Here they were to board the much slower, and considerably more noisy, stormboats. While the Royal Marines were to make a swift, direct crossing to take the enemy on the far shore by surprise, the men of 6 Commando were hoping that their noisy craft might help create some confusion amongst the Germans on the far side as to just where the landings were taking place.

While the commandos made their preparations, the continuous artillery bombardment that had been pounding the far shore from Emerich to Wesel since 1800hrs, continued unabated. At 2150hrs, XII Corps guns switched their concentrations to the Grav Insel and the area to the west of Wesel, softening up the landing places of the commando assault. Around the same time, the stormboats started their engines and began moving down the creek that led out onto the Rhine. The noise and the movement of the boats immediately attracted enemy fire. Just short of the river, the craft pulled over and embarked the men of 6 Commando while German shells continued crashing amongst them. At 2200hrs the stormboats began to move out into the Rhine to start their long crossing.

Upstream the Buffaloes carrying 46 RM Commando and Brigade HQ rose up over the five-metre-high dykes bordering the river, revved their engines and then plunged down into the water to start their dash to the far side. It took between three and four minutes to make the crossings

Duplex Drive (DD) Sherman tanks of 44th Royal Tank Regiment, part of 4th Armoured Brigade) are launched from the Allied side of the Rhine to cross the river in support of 15th (Scottish) Division. The photo was taken early morning of 24 March. (BU 2172, IWM)

during which time one Buffalo was hit and burst into flames. Just four of the men inside managed to get out. The other amphibious craft pressed on to the enemy-held shore and drove up out of the water scattering the dazed German defenders. Within a short time the two leading troops had fanned out inland, seeking the objectives they had studied for weeks. The strongest resistance was found to be around two waterman's cottages, the first of which was located 600 metres from the shore. This small fortress was taken with only minimal casualties, but the second, 400 metres to the east, required the assistance of some of the men of the two follow-up troops of the commando. Other men moved to the left and attacked a flak position, while still more Royal Marines swept the small 'island' clear of the enemy.

Downstream of 46 RM Commando, the men of 6 Commando had a very torrid crossing. Although their stormboats had a fairly low profile, their noise made them easy for the enemy to locate. Many of the boats were sunk by German small-arms fire, flinging their occupants into the icy water. Still more were rendered useless by engine failure. Fortunately for the men struggling in the water, Brig Mills Roberts had insisted that small dories be included in the assault to act as lifeboats. These tiny craft now began fishing men out of the river and snatching them to safety from stricken stormboats. In spite of these troubles, most of 6 Commando were able to reach the forming-up point on Grav Insel and prepare for the move on Wesel. Once assembled, they headed eastwards towards the town so as to be ready to exploit the tactical support that was to be supplied by the RAF, marking out a route through the minefields with white tape as they went. Back on the river, the surviving Buffaloes had returned to the friendly shore and were ferrying over both 45 Royal Marine and 3 Commando.

At 2215hrs, the pathfinders of RAF Bomber Command swept low over Wesel, dropping marking flares on the soon-to-be-obliterated town. By this time in the war Bomber Command had acquired considerable experience of ground-support operations. The saturation bombing of a target so close to the commando positions nonetheless caused some concern, for the operation required very precise control. At 2230hrs, Lancaster bombers began their raid and for the next 15 minutes unleashed 1,100 tons of high explosive on the town. The special troops of 1st Commando Brigade watched with awe as the terrifying spectacle unfolded just 1,000 metres in front of the lead troops. The ground shook as though by earthquakes. Then, as the last of the Lancasters turned for home, the shaken and dazed men of 6 Commando pressed on through the smoke and dust to complete a safe route into the town for the remainder of the brigade. Wesel had been reduced to a mass of rubble and burning buildings. It seemed impossible that anyone could have survived the bombing, but survive they did, and the German troops of 180th Division, and the various anti-aircraft and support units holding the town now readied themselves and their guns for the inevitable British attack.

The landings by 1st Commando Brigade and the heavy bombing raid on Wesel had convinced GenMaj Bernhard Klosterkemper that the crossings in his division's sector were not a feint. He alerted his corps commander, Gen d.Inf Erich Straube, as to the strength and direction of the commando attack and called for reinforcements. Meanwhile he concentrated all available artillery on the commando lodgement. At LXXXVI Corps' HQ, Straube relayed the bad news to the army commander and readied the few troops that he had as his reserve to be sent against Wesel. At First Parachute Army's headquarters, Gen d. Fallschirm Alfred Schlemm now had to contend with two separate crossings of the Rhine spaced around 16 kilometres apart, one at Rees and another at Wesel. Both caused concern, but the attack on Wesel seemed to be the most critical, for the loss of the town and its road network would hamper any attempts to switch his defensive forces. It had to be dealt with.

The heavy defensive fire put down on 1st Commando Brigade's landing places by Klosterkemper had been too late. Most of the brigade had moved eastwards and was now attacking Wesel. The shell and mortar fire that fell along the near empty river bank interfered with the supply lines, but did not slow down the attack on the town.

By midnight the whole of 1st Commando Brigade was involved in the clearing of Wesel. Pockets of German resistance were found along almost every street, but few of the dazed defenders were able to hold out for long against skilful infiltration by elite troops. An hour later elements of the entire brigade had reached the centre of the town and set about digging in. There was still plenty of enemy resistance in the south of Wesel, but most of those German defenders were now trapped against the Rhine and the River Lippe. The main threat to the commandos would be from the landward side to the north. Brig Mills Roberts now ordered two columns to move northwards along the two main streets to the edge of the town and for 45 RM Commando to move ahead to take the known resistance point based around the wire factory. These moves were completed against sporadic resistance at around 0200hrs. Once 45 RM Commando had consolidated on its final objective, its men strengthened their positions with all means available, waiting for the inevitable German counterattack. Orders were to hold until relieved by airborne troops.

The first attack came at 45 RM Commando during the night. A self-propelled gun backed by infantry got close to its lines but was turned back by the Royal Marines. The gun remained in the area of the cemetery, sniping at the commando for the rest of the night. A short while later, all of the four commandos heard the sound of tracked vehicles. Gen Straube had ordered the few German tanks that he had in reserve north of Wesel against the British troops in the town. They used a small copse north of the town as a forming-up point. Each of the

THE 15TH (SCOTTISH) DIVISION REINFORCES ITS BRIDGEHEAD ACROSS THE RIVER RHINE ON THE MORNING OF 24 MARCH 1945. (Pages 38–39)

The right hand division of British Second Army opened its attack across the River Rhine opposite the village of Bislich, four miles downstream of Wesel, with a two-battalion crossing by 44th Brigade at 0200 hrs on 24 March. Enemy resistance to 15th (Scottish) Division's assault was fairly light and none of its craft was hit while on the river. A bridgehead was soon formed and the lead battalions were able to move quickly inland, taking Bislich (1) within the first few hours. Just after first light, the 44th Brigade brought over its follow up battalion, 6th King's Own Scottish Borderers, to reinforce the two lead battalions and help to enlarge the lodgement. The scene shows the Scottish Borderers making their crossing. Some German mortar and artillery fire is falling on the river, but most of the enemy have been pushed back from the river and are defending small villages a mile or so inland. Buffaloes (tracked amphibious vehicles) and stormboats were available to the Scottish Division to carry men across the river. By the time of the River Rhine operation, Buffaloes (2) were in common use by lead companies making an assault river crossing. Earlier attempts to cross waterways under fire, such as the River Seine crossings in August 1944, had relied on ungainly Stormboats (3) to force a passage and casualties from enemy fire had been high. Stormboats were a much more vulnerable method of carrying men across water. These open plywood craft had no protection, were extremely heavy and cumbersome to manoeuvre when out of the water – it took 36 men to carry each of them – and troops had to embark directly onto the craft at the water's edge, often under fire. Powered by a single Evinrude outboard motor, they could reach a speed of six knots when loaded to a maximum capacity of eighteen men. Stormboats were used by the Scottish Division to carry over the follow up troops after the main assault when events on the river were a little more quiet. The use of Buffaloes in the assault was a much safer method. They were able to be fully loaded in sheltered areas way back from the river, away from interference by the enemy. They could then move directly across open ground, down to the watercourse and out into open water without pause. The men inside were given some protection from small arms fire by the steel construction of the craft as they cruised across at a speed of seven knots. Both assault battalions of 44th Brigade used Buffaloes from 79th Armoured Division to carry over their attack companies. The craft were then given over to the shipping of guns and transport into the bridgehead. Also crossing at this time were a number of Duplex Drive (DD) Sherman tanks (4) from 44th Royal Tank Regiment of 79th Armoured Division. Their low profile whilst on the water made them very difficult targets for enemy guns. Once ashore, they would drop their canvas flotation skirts and assume the role of a normal gun tank. The DD Sherman was an excellent solution to the problem of getting tanks across to support lead troops before any bridges could be built.

commandos located this area by sound and passed back map references to the guns of XII Corps which were still on call to the brigade. A few minutes later the small wood and the surrounding area was plastered by hundreds of shells. The enemy attack was broken up in disorder and the setback to Straube's forces deterred them from mounting another large-scale attack that night.

15th (SCOTTISH) DIVISION

Operation *Plunder* was well under way by the time that 15th (Scottish) Division was introduced into the battle with its own Operation *Torchlight*. With troops across and established on the two extreme flanks of Second Army's sector, it was time to attack in the centre. The Scottish Division planned to cross the Rhine on a two-brigade front with four battalions in the assault. On the right, north-east of Xanten, 44th Brigade would cross with 6th Royal Scots Fusiliers and 8th Royal Scots, while on the left 227th Brigade would attack from the area of Vynen with 2nd Argyll and Sutherland Highlanders and 10th Highland Light Infantry.

The guns of XII corps had been firing across the river with their counter-battery programme since 1700hrs on 23 March. At 2330hrs, those of the 15th Division concentrated on the enemy positions immediately opposite. At 0100hrs the next morning, a 'pepper pot' of fire which included every type of gun in the division and corps – heavies, mediums, field, anti-aircraft, anti-tank, light cannons right down to 0.5in machine guns – all plastered the far shore with high explosive and tracer. In reply, a few shells and one or two flickering lines of machine-gun fire came back from the enemy side of the river.

At exactly 0200hrs the two Scottish brigades launched their attack. Amphibious Buffaloes manned by the 11th Royal Tanks and the East

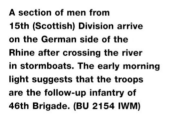

A section of men from 15th (Scottish) Division arrive on the German side of the Rhine after crossing the river in stormboats. The early morning light suggests that the troops are the follow-up infantry of 46th Brigade. (BU 2154 IWM)

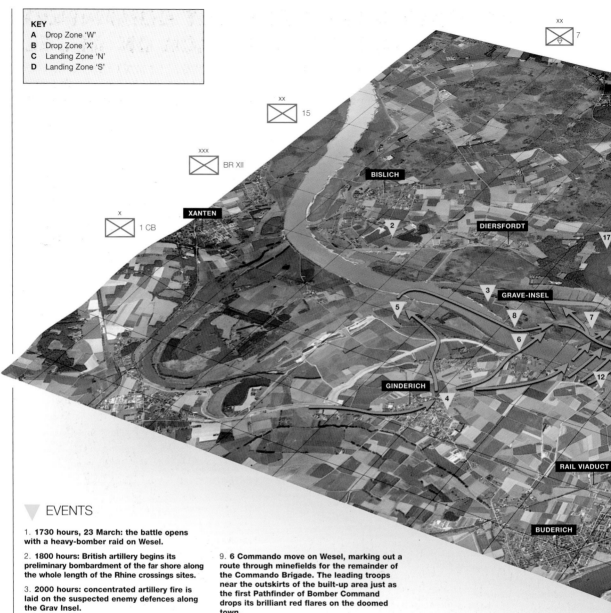

KEY
A Drop Zone 'W'
B Drop Zone 'X'
C Landing Zone 'N'
D Landing Zone 'S'

XX
7

XX
15

XXX
BR XII

X
1 CB

XANTEN

BISLICH

DIERSFORDT

17

2

3 GRAVE-INSEL

5

8

7

6

12

GINDERICH

4

RAIL VIADUCT

BUDERICH

▼ EVENTS

1. **1730 hours, 23 March: the battle opens with a heavy-bomber raid on Wesel.**

2. **1800 hours: British artillery begins its preliminary bombardment of the far shore along the whole length of the Rhine crossings sites.**

3. **2000 hours: concentrated artillery fire is laid on the suspected enemy defences along the Grav Insel.**

4. **2130 hours: 46 RM Commando and 1st Commando Brigade Tactical HQ board Buffalos and begin their forward move to the Rhine.**

5. **2130 hours: 6 Commando begin their embarkation onto the stormboats provided by 84 Field Company RE. Their noisy engines alert the enemy and attract German fire.**

6. **2200 hours: 46 RM Commando begins its assault crossing, covered by a barrage of artillery fire. Enemy fire destroys one Buffalo during the crossing, but the majority of the two leading Troops get ashore without loss.**

7. **B and Y Troops of 46 RM Commando sweep inland and attack the strongholds surrounding two Watermen's Houses 600 metres from the shore. After fierce fighting, the stronghold is taken and Grav Insel secured.**

8. **A and Z Troops of 46 RM Commando reinforce the small bridgehead and are joined by 6 Commando landing from stormboats.**

9. **6 Commando move on Wesel, marking out a route through minefields for the remainder of the Commando Brigade. The leading troops near the outskirts of the built-up area just as the first Pathfinder of Bomber Command drops its brilliant red flares on the doomed town.**

10. **2230 hours: 250 heavy bombers from the RAF obliterate Wesel and all of its buildings.**

11. **2245 hours: just as the Lancaster bombers turn away, 6 Commando move into the burning town, marking a safe route as they go.**

12. **2300 hours: returning Buffalos bring 45 RM and 3 Commandos across the river.**

13. **2400 hours: all four Commandos are into the town clearing it of the enemy. 45 RM Commando moves northwards and seizes the Wire Factory to anchor the brigade's northern flank.**

14. **Throughout the night, several German attacks, two supported by tanks, are beaten off.**

15. **3, 6 and 46 RM Commandos sweep the town towards the south and force the remaining German defenders into a pocket near the River Lippe.**

16. **At daybreak on 24 March, 1st Cheshires cross the Rhine near the blown rail bridge and help the commandos clear the southern part of Wesel.**

17. **1000 hours: US XVIII Corps' airborne landings begin and by 1100 hours the troops of US 194th Glider Infantry are moving toward their objectives.**

18. **Around midday, a patrol from 3 Commando makes contact with US glider-borne troops to link together the airborne and river assaults across the Rhine.**

OPERATION *WIDGEON*: 1ST COMMANDO BRIGADE'S ATTACK ON WESEL

The early capture of the communications centre of Wesel was vital to the success of Operation *Plunder* but it had a large German garrison. The town was first to be obliterated by heavy bombers and then cleared by a commando brigade, until relieved.

Note: Gridlines are shown at intervals of 1 km (1093 yds)

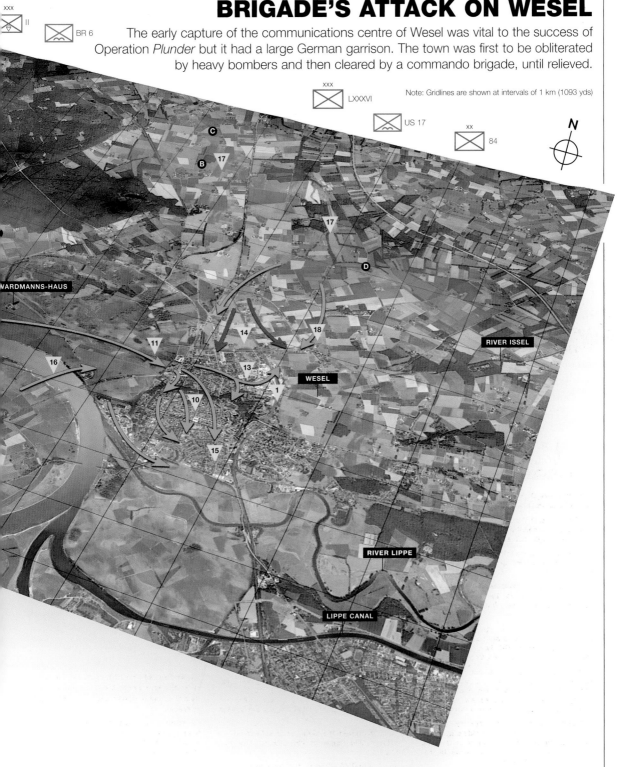

Riding Yeomanry led the way, with follow-up troops crossing in stormboats. During 44th Brigade's crossings not one Buffalo was hit and all of the craft carrying the two assault battalions reached their chosen landing places. The first casualties were from small-arms fire and mines. It was inevitable that anti-personnel 'schu' mines would claim a number of victims for they had been liberally sown all along the far bank of the Rhine. Unhappily, more casualties were suffered by the Royal Scots Fusiliers from friendly shellfire than from the enemy; two shells fell short amongst D Company and knocked out over twenty men.

With little opposition on the enemy shoreline to deal with, the two battalions quickly moved along the high bund that lined the river, clearing it of German defenders. Within just two hours they had cleared three kilometres of river bank and had troops on the outskirts of Bislich and Loh. By this time the 6th King's Own Scottish Borderers had completed their crossing in stormboats and were preparing to move through the Royal Scots Fusiliers to take Bislich. Just before dawn on the 6th, King's Own Scottish Borderers put in its attack and seized the village.

Once the far shore had been cleared of the enemy, the river could be given over to the build-up. Buffaloes began ferrying over guns and

The landing place of 46 Royal Marine Commando on Grav Insel. The commando came ashore just after 2130hrs on 23 March. (Ken Ford)

carriers and engineers were able to start the preparatory work associated with bridge building. DD tanks now took to the water to begin the task of getting armour into the bridgehead. At first light these tanks went into action when a squadron of DD Shermans from 44th Royal Tanks supported the Royal Scots in their attack on Vissel and Jöckern which were taken against negligible resistance.

The other formation of 15th Division assaulting the Rhine that morning was 227th Brigade. Its attack went a little less smoothly than its sister brigade, the 44th. The two lead battalions entered the water at 0200hrs as planned: the 2nd Argylls crossed the river on the left just north of Vynen with the 10th Highland Light Infantry on the right three kilometres farther upstream.

The 10th HLI's passage across the Rhine was relatively quiet, but unfortunately it was not accurate. Both of its lead companies found themselves farther upstream than intended and were quickly engaged by almost a battalion of German paratroopers when they tried to clear the bund along the river and move inland. Confused and bitter fighting followed in which A Company lost all of its officers. The battalion's two follow-up companies also landed in the same wrong location and compounded the confusion. Much of the enemy resistance seemed to be located in Overkamp and things on the river bank did not settle down until the HLI put in a battalion attack on the village and cleared it of the enemy.

Three kilometres downstream of the 10th HLI was the crossing place of the 2nd Argyll and Sutherland Highlanders. It, too, had difficulties with its landing places, causing one of its companies to be split up either side of an inlet. German paratroopers were in evidence along the bunds and in the scattered villages a kilometre or so inland. Fire from these villages interfered with the build-up and continued to hamper operations until the Argylls moved against them. Help was at hand when a company of 2nd Gordon Highlanders crossed over at around 0600hrs and moved north-eastwards to help take Lohr. The brigade commander, Brig Colville,

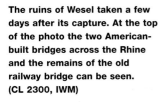

The ruins of Wesel taken a few days after its capture. At the top of the photo the two American-built bridges across the Rhine and the remains of the old railway bridge can be seen. (CL 2300, IWM)

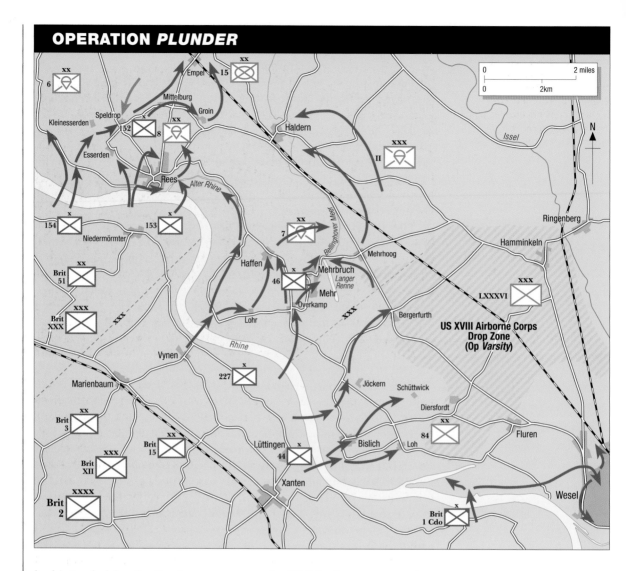

had intended for the Gordons to support the HLI farther upstream, but the need to clear the Argyll sector was more pressing, for until Lohr was captured resupply and engineering work on the river would have to be delayed. The village finally fell after a prolonged attack which involved very difficult house-to-house clearance. The paratroopers defending the place finally withdrew when DD tanks came up to support the Argylls.

THE FIRST MORNING

Everyone in British Second Army was elated when daylight came on 24 March, for it was soon obvious that the lodgement gained on the far side of the Rhine was well established, casualties had been relatively light and progress inland was beginning to gather pace. FM Montgomery was satisfied with the night's work. Everyone now waited to see how the enemy would react.

On the left flank of the operation, however, things were beginning to prove difficult for the 51st (Highland) Division. When news of the

Men from a support troop from one of the commandos in Wesel man their Vickers machine guns on the northern outskirts of Wesel. The photograph was taken on the morning after the assault as the commandos waited to make contact with airborne troops. (BU 2329, IWM)

division's crossings had reached German Army Group H's commander, Gen Blaskowitz, he realized that this was almost certainly not the main Allied assault. Nevertheless the risk to the road network through Rees was great and needed removing. Blaskowitz decided to release 15th Panzer Grenadier Division from his reserve and send it immediately against the Highland Division in the hope of throwing back this first assault before the main attack could begin. The Highland Division felt this increase in enemy resistance when it was forced to deal with an enemy counterattack against Speldrop. The strength of the German attack was such that the 1st Black Watch was evicted from the village and withdrew to Kleinesserden. Fighting went on well into the day and the situation was not fully restored until the Highland Light Infantry of Canada – attached to 154th Brigade from Canadian 9th Brigade for the operation – were introduced into the battle. Further strong counter-attacks were endured by 7th Black Watch, holding the left flank of the river line, and by the 7th Argylls, who were trying to expand the bridgehead north-west towards Bienen.

The Highland Division's other assault brigade, 153rd Brigade, was involved in clearing Rees and was fully occupied removing the paratroopers of German 8th Parachute Division from the town. The follow-up brigade, 152nd Brigade, caught some of the counterattack of 15th Panzer Grenadier Division as its 2nd Seaforth and 5th Camerons tried to advance on Mittelburg. The two battalions had been held up by an anti-tank ditch north of Rees. A squadron of DD Shermans from the Staffordshire Yeomanry helped the infantry breach the ditch later in the morning, but four of these tanks were later knocked out and enemy resistance was such that the advance stalled.

On 15th Scottish Division's front, enemy resistance consisted of the bulk of German 7th Parachute Division. Again, once the river line had been breached, the paratroopers based their defence in and around the

Commandos in Wesel seem pleased with their 'bag' of German prisoners. The captives themselves also appear relieved to be out of the battle. (BU 2315, IWM)

hamlets and villages that lay back from the Rhine. Enemy opposition at each of these points was substantial, as was to be expected from German airborne troops, but heavy support for the Scottish infantry was on immediate call from the massed artillery across the river, from fighter bombers in the air and from increasing numbers of tanks on the ground. This support, however, began to fade as the time drew near for the fly-in by US XVIII Airborne Corps. At around 0930hrs a halt was called to all artillery fire across the river and all fighter-bomber operations.

On the left of the Scottish Division, 227th Brigade applied its strength, pushing through the scattered hamlets near the river towards a link-up with 51st Division. In the centre, 46th Brigade moved north-westerly, attempting to clear the villages of Mehr and Haffen. On the right, 44th Brigade had the important task of carving a route towards Burgerfurth to meet up with both British airborne troops on the edge of the Diersfordter Forest, and with American airborne troops near the village of Diersfordt.

In Wesel, 1st Commando Brigade had spent the night dealing with the enemy. In the north of the town the Germans probed the commando positions with counterattacks of varying strength. Some were backed by one or two tanks, whilst others were made by small groups of infantry attempting to infiltrate the widely spaced groups of commandos. All attacks were successfully held. In the south of the town, street clearing went on against tired and dispirited enemy groups. The German commander of the Wesel garrison, GenMaj Friedrich Deutsch, was killed in the process of being evicted from his headquarters. Everyone in Wesel now waited for the arrival of the airborne assault and the link-up with US 17th Airborne Division.

Troops of 1st Cheshire Regiment arrive on the banks of the Rhine beside Wesel on the morning after the assault to support 1st Commando Brigade's hold on the town. The ruins of the old railway bridge can be seen in the background. (BU 2336, IWM)

THE AMERICAN ASSAULT

he weight of arms that British Second Army put into the assault in Operation *Plunder*, was almost mirrored in the south by US Ninth Army for its attack across the river in Operation *Flashpoint*. Unlike Lt Gen Miles Dempsey, however, Lt Gen Bill Simpson intended to use a single corps in his assault, but a corps that had been enlarged almost to army strength.

Simpson chose the most inexperienced of his three corps, XVI Corps, commanded by Maj Gen John Anderson, for the attack. Having been introduced into combat late in February on the River Roer crossings, XVI Corps then took part in the drive to the Rhine. For the assault itself, Anderson chose to rely on two of his most experienced divisions, 30th and 79th Infantry Divisions, both of which had been in action since France the previous June with other corps. Following up after the assault were the 35th and 75th Divisions, with 8th Armored Division providing the tanks to back up the infantry and add punch to the subsequent breakout. The 35th Infantry Division was also a veteran of the Normandy campaign, whilst the 75th Division had had its baptism of fire during the Ardennes offensive in December 1944. The newest of all these units was 8th Armored Division, which had seen its first action only two months previously during the fighting in the south to clear the Saar–Moselle triangle.

These five divisions were swelled in numbers by the addition of further artillery and tank groups. Anderson also received command of the 34th Field Artillery Brigade containing 13 battalions of medium, heavy and

Prime Minister Winston Churchill, FM Alanbrooke and FM Montgomery ride across the Rhine in a landing craft. The group were visiting US Ninth Army's bridgehead with Lt Gen Simpson and some of his commanders. Prominent in the front of the photo are Maj Gen Anderson (US XVI Corps) on the left and Maj Gen Wyche (79th Division) on the right. (BU 2248, IWM)

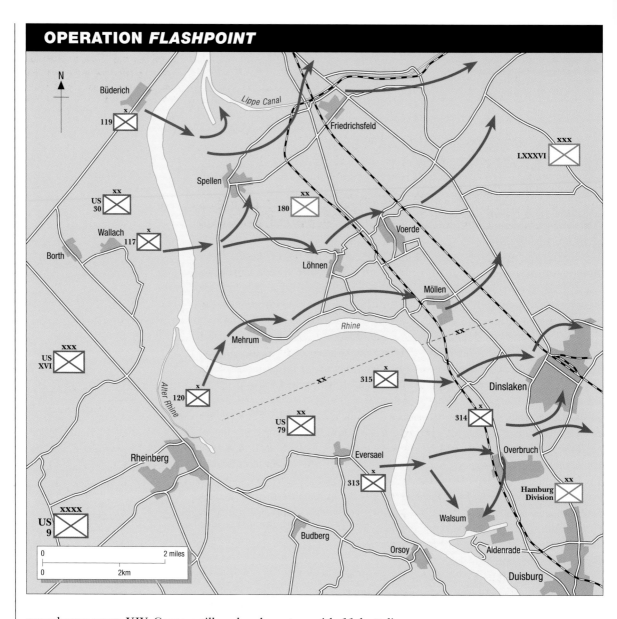

superheavy guns; XIX Corps artillery headquarters with 11 battalions; a tank-destroyer group with six battalions; six other separate tank battalions; three engineering combat groups; two anti-aircraft groups; a smoke-generator battalion; a chemical (4.2in mortar) battalion and a number of smaller units which included several naval contingencies. This raised the strength of XVI Corps to over 120,000 men, with 54 field battalions of artillery in support.

Supporting US Ninth Army from the air was Brig Gen Richard Nugent's US XXIX Tactical Air Command. This command would provide a fighter-bomber group to work with each of the assault divisions (373rd Fighter-Bomber Group with 79th Division and 366th Fighter-Bomber Group with 30th Division) as well as providing support and cover to the daylight attack by US XVIII Airborne Corps. Two days prior to the crossings, a programme of neutralizing the *Luftwaffe* was implemented, with heavy attacks on ten German airfields immediately north of Twenty-

First Army Group's sector of the Rhine. A larger interdiction programme had begun in the last week of February by the RAF and the US Eighth Air Force which used over 1,000 heavy bombers in a series of attacks against important bridges, viaducts, railways and road networks from Koblenz to the North Sea.

With so much artillery and air power available to the XVI Corps, it is not surprising that each assault division was well supported. In addition to its own artillery, the 30th Division had three extra battalions of field guns and the artillery of 35th Division attached, making a total of 11 field artillery battalions directly under command. Likewise with 79th Division, it had three non-divisional battalions and the guns of 8th Armoured division attached, giving it ten battalions of guns on call.

The guns available to XVI Corps were designed to be put to good use in the coming battle, for the fire plan was extremely comprehensive. Prior intelligence had located a great number of enemy targets to be engaged during Operation *Flashpoint*, 989 in total. These included 54 definite and 68 probable German gun batteries; 52 command posts; 36 supply depots or dumps; 42 German observation posts; 24 possible assembly areas; 454 locations for interdictory fire and 258 miscellaneous targets of opportunity.

The plan called for a programme of scheduled fire to begin at 0100hrs until 1000hrs (the time of the airborne attack) on the day of the assault. After that, fire was as requested or as observed. It would start with one hour of extremely heavy bombardment prior to the assault, then three hours of heavy scheduled fire in support of the attacking troops during the hours of darkness and, finally, artillery fire would be either on call or scheduled fire. Prodigious amounts of ammunition had been stockpiled for the attack, most of which was used as planned. During the first hour-long preparation phase, 65,261 rounds were fired. In the next four hours this figure was doubled to a total of 131,450 rounds.

Lt Gen Simpson had decided to hold the line of the Rhine with his XIII Corps (Maj Gen Alvan Gillem) while XVI Corps concentrated for the attack. Maj Gen Raymond McLain's XIX Corps was to assemble in the rear, ready to come forward and cross into the bridgehead at the earliest possible date to add momentum to the breakout. Gillem's corps would then continue to hold the area to the west of the Rhine until released by the arrival of the newly raised US Fifteenth Army (Lt Gen Leonard Gerow).

Maj Gen Anderson's plan for the attack was to assault on a two-division front, with 30th Division crossing on the left, upstream of Wesel, and 79th Division on the right, east of Rheinberg. All three regiments of 30th Division and two of 79th Division would take part in the assault. The initial two waves would cross in stormboats and subsequent waves in double assault boats. Follow-up waves would be made in any stormboats and assault boats that were still in operation and in tracked landing vehicles (LVTs) – known to the British as 'Buffaloes' – and on landing craft vehicle and personnel (LCVPs) manned by the US Navy. Support weapons and supplies would be carried over after the assault in landing craft medium (LCMs), LCVPs and in DUKWs. Until bridges were built, tanks and tank destroyers, with the exception of amphibious DD tanks, would be ferried over by raft.

30th INFANTRY DIVISION

At 0100hrs on 24 March, 40,000 American artillerymen went into action and launched US Ninth Army's assault across the River Rhine, firing an hour-long bombardment at German positions on the far side of the water. Just before 0200hrs, outboard motors began to cough into life and the infantry of three battalions filed down to the waterfront to get on board their waiting stormboats. Overhead, the thunderous barrage continued unabated. In reply, a few enemy shells shrieked across the sky, one or two ribbons of tracer snaked across the river and an occasional mortar round sent up plumes of water.

Farthest downstream of 30th Division's assault groups, the lead battalion of 119th Infantry Regiment began taking to the water just south-east of the village of Buderich. Its objective on the far shore was the area above the confluence of the Rhine and the Lippe rivers. The 54 stormboats carrying the first waves of the battalion each carried seven men and a crew of two. Soon the boats' 55hp motors were screaming at full pitch as the craft pulled out into midstream and the assault began, their paths guided by machine guns firing tracer bullets at their landing places on the far side – further waves would be guided ashore by coloured aircraft landing lights.

When they reached mid-river away from the grey smoke which shielded the near shore, enemy fire began to home in on them, knocking out two stormboats, killing one man and wounding three others. A few minutes later the stormboats struck bottom and their troops piled out, rushing up the high bund which lined the river, spraying the ground ahead with machine-pistol fire. At this point the artillery fire lifted away from the river front to engage targets farther inland, the move indicated to the infantry by the firing of white phosphorus. There were few of the enemy still competent to put up any opposition; those that manned the river positions and had survived the bombardment had had the fight knocked out of them. The 119th Regiment had made a virtually unopposed crossing.

The same was true for the other two regiments of 30th Division. The 117th Regiment had crossed from the riverbank alongside Wallach and had made landfall alongside the enemy-held village of Ork against negligible opposition, although one German position on the top of the bund had the temerity to fire on the boats as they came ashore. This post was quickly eliminated. Farther upstream, from the vicinity of a big bend in the river north-east of Rheinberg, 120th Infantry Regiment crossed over without loss.

All three regiments of Maj Gen Hobb's 30th Division now began the task of capturing the villages set back from the river. Little hard fighting was involved in wresting these places from those of the German 180th Division who were charged with defending them and GenMaj Klosterkemper had little in reserve to send to their aid. He was too preoccupied with clearing British 1st Commando Brigade from Wesel. Within two hours of the start, 30th Division had captured Spellen, Ork and Mehrum and had cleared the complete river bank in its sector. All three regiments had two battalions over the river and a platoon of DD tanks had crossed over to help 117th Regiment in the centre of the bridgehead. In view of the hazards, casualties had been remarkably light.

The first serious opposition to the division was met in the mid-morning by 119th Regiment when it tried to get under a bridge beneath the industrial railway line which led up from the docks at Walsum. Just outside Friedrichsfeld the enemy had established a roadblock across the

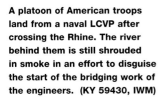

A platoon of American troops land from a naval LCVP after crossing the Rhine. The river behind them is still shrouded in smoke in an effort to disguise the start of the bridging work of the engineers. (KY 59430, IWM)

American advance. Progress was stalled until a few light tanks were ferried over the river in LCMs and came up to join the infantry. After a stiff battle, a way was forged past the obstacle and the 119th began to clear Friedrichsfeld then to advance over the second rail line which linked Wesel and Dinslaken. On the left of the regiment, a spit of land between the Lippe Canal and the River Lippe just above Wesel held several anti-aircraft batteries that had not been eliminated. These gun sites continued to be troublesome until Gen Hobbs dispatched two companies to deal with them. Crossing the canal farther to the east, the Americans eliminated the flak guns by an attack from the rear. They then moved back up the river bank to clear along the River Lippe and establish American positions overlooking Wesel.

Troops of the 117th Regiment also encountered stiff enemy resistance when they moved eastwards and tried to pass beneath the first railway line north of Voerde. A cratered road covered by a well established anti-tank gun blocked their path and proved difficult to eliminate. The way was finally opened when supporting artillery blasted the roadblock apart. By the end of the day, the 117th Regiment had troops across the second railway line and dug in amongst the open fields beyond, bracing themselves for the inevitable German counterattack.

On the right of the division, 120th Regiment swung round the great bend in the Rhine and took Möllen astride the first railway line. In the afternoon its 3rd Battalion was joined by Sherman tanks and some tank destroyers and pressed on eastwards to cross the second rail line and the main road from Dinslaken to Wesel. When its lead battalion reached open ground it came under heavy shellfire, not from the enemy, but from the US 79th Division on its right. The rapid progress made by the 120th Regiment had brought it abreast of Maj Gen Wyche's division before anyone had thought possible and the 79th Division assumed that its troops were the enemy. Fortunately casualties were light and Maj Mucullough's battalion continued inland against negligible opposition. It halted when ten kilometres from its crossing place, at the limit of effective direct artillery fire from across the river.

79th INFANTRY DIVISION

The last of Twenty-First Army Group's amphibious assaults across the River Rhine was made by US 79th Division. Its start time was an hour after that of 30th Division's at 0300hrs. The extra hour was made because of the location of the attack. The great loops of the Rhine east of Rheinberg meant that the proposed landing places of 79th Division were four kilometres east of those made by 30th Division. The delayed start time meant that Hobbs' division had extra time to advance eastwards to come abreast of 79th Division and close its open right flank before Wyche's division attacked. It also meant that 79th Division would have two hours of pre-assault bombardment instead of one.

Maj Gen Wyche had chosen to make his assault with two of his three regiments, each with one battalion in the attack. The 315th Infantry Regiment was to cross from Milchplatz to make a landing just upstream of Möllen, while the 313th Infantry Regiment would go across from the area of Eversael. Wyche chose a mix of stormboats and assault boats in

the attack, with the slower assault boats kicking off first and the faster stormboats following a few minutes later.

When the first battalion of 315th Regiment took to the water at 0300hrs the river was clouded with a mixture of fog and smoke, making station-keeping difficult for the boats on the river. Direction was lost and some units became scattered and confused. The men in these craft lost their way altogether and returned to the home shore thinking they had crossed the Rhine. Here they were surprised to find other American troops of the follow-up wave coming towards them to board their boats. Those infantry that did get across did so against light opposition and suffered few casualties, with the artillery support rising from the enemy bank only when the stormboats and assault craft were three quarters of the way across. Those of the enemy that were still at their posts along the dykes bordering the river were found by the Americans to be in the words of one infantryman: 'completely stunned, scared and shook up; they had never encountered anything like it.'

With little opposition along the river line, the infantry swept inland and reached the first railway line in record time. While the next battalion crossed the Rhine behind them, the momentum of the advance carried the leading troops of 313th Regiment right to the outskirts of Dinslaken two kilometres away, a town with a peacetime population of 25,000. Nowhere did the Germans exercise more than just token resistance at any defensible position.

Crossing a little farther south from the area along the river bank by Eversael, was Wyche's 313th Regiment. Like its sister regiment two kilometres to the north, its passage across the river was uneventful. The lead battalion swarmed over the bund, clearing out the dazed enemy that had remained, then swiftly moved inland to the first railway. Once across, it swung south-eastwards, cleared Overbruch and then held position whilst the follow-up battalion took over the advance and moved on to Walsum. Throughout the day the regiment consolidated this position in Walsum and built up a flank defence for the division along the town's canal and harbour. Casualties for the day: one man killed and 11 wounded.

When the division's third regiment had crossed over the river, Maj Gen Wyche pushed his troops as far inland as was practicable. The 314th Regiment, with tank and tank-destroyer support, expanded the bridgehead beyond Dinslaken over the second railway and took up positions three kilometres into open country.

An American bulldozer pushes a naval landing craft containing an M18 MGC (Motor Gun Carriage) 'Hellcat', away from the near shore, prior to crossing into US Ninth Army's bridgehead. The silhouette of the Hellcat's long 76mm M1 gun can be clearly seen. The M18 was one of the finest tank destroyers of the war and saw action in both Italy and north-west Europe. (EN 59398, IWM)

By the end of the first day, Anderson's XVI Corps had a bridgehead 16 kilometres long and eight kilometres deep, anchored on both flanks by a canal line. Enemy opposition had been slight, allowing both attacking divisions to carve out room to manoeuvre and gather strength. Casualties in the corps were remarkably light for such a momentous undertaking: 41 killed, 450 wounded and seven missing. The German troops that were stationed in the area could only put up a dispirited and ineffectual defence, over 2,100 of them had been taken prisoner. American 79th Division had struck on the junction between German 180th Division of LXXXVI Corps and the Hamburg Division of LXIII Corps and had split the two apart. The enemy was unable to organize a solid front under the weight of the impact. GenMaj Abraham, commander of LXIII Corps, knew that the low-rated *Volksturm* groups from the Hamburg Division would never be able to stop the Americans now that they were ashore, so he decided to move his 2nd Parachute Division northwards from its section of the Rhine below Duisburg as yet untouched by the American attack. Anderson's XVI Corps would now have to deal with much stiffer opposition. But that was to take effect the next day, the most pressing task now was to move artillery and armour into the bridgehead to support the expansion of the lodgement ready for the breakout. To do this Anderson needed bridges.

Immediately after the assault battalions had swept across the Rhine, engineering work began on the near shore to build bridges on both divisions' fronts. Great gaps were blown in the high winter dyke that lay inland and routes down to the water were constructed from prefabricated road material that had been stockpiled a short way to the rear. Every available truck was pressed into action to bring the component parts forward so that approach roads could be built. Work started simultaneously constructing ramps for the bridges and launching sites for the rafts.

Originally it had been intended that work to erect bridges across the Rhine would only start when the bridgehead had expanded far enough to eliminate observed enemy artillery fire on the bridging sites. This intention was reconsidered when news filtered back that enemy resistance was lighter than expected. As good quantities of smoke were still available to conceal the construction sites, the signal was given during the early morning to start the lengthy task of building the bridges. In the meantime, work would continue assembling Bailey 40-ton rafts to carry tanks across and small 9-ton treadway rafts to convey lighter guns and transport. By noon on the first day, 30th Division had two Bailey rafts as well as several treadway rafts in operation, while 79th Division's first Bailey raft had been completed an hour earlier. Altogether five 40-ton rafts were built by the end of the first day, allowing XVI Corps to ferry one Sherman tank across every ten minutes.

Engineers began constructing US 30th Division's first bridge just four hours after the assault began. At 0600hrs, work was started on a float-reinforced 25-ton pontoon bridge. It was sited at Wallach in the centre of the division's zone, well away from observed enemy fire. The 350m bridge was ready for service at 0100hrs the next morning. The 338m treadway bridge that was begun at 0630hrs at Mehrum was less successful. Construction was delayed by enemy shellfire which knocked out 44m of the bridge. The next morning a naval craft collided with the bridge, destroying its alignment and caused further delays. Eventually it was open for traffic at 1700hrs on 25 March. The most remarkable engineering achievement was the construction of a treadway bridge at Wallach. It was begun at 0630hrs on the first day. At 0815hrs all treadway rafts in service on that part of the river were called back by the engineers to be incorporated into the bridge. Work continued at a furious pace that day and at 1600hrs in the afternoon the engineers were proudly able to declare it open for human traffic. It was later damaged by an out-of-control Bailey raft which drifted into it.

The 79th Division's engineers were less lucky, for enemy fire continued to interfere with their sites throughout the day. Construction on the 384m bridge at Milchplatz began at 0800hrs. Intermittent enemy shells crashed down around the bridging site throughout the whole of its construction. Further impediment to the work occurred when three loose LCMs drifted downstream and swept away 145 metres of the finished bridge. The work was finally completed during the afternoon of 26 March.

Late on 25 March work began on the approaches to two Bailey floating bridges, one at Mehrum and one at Wallach. Construction of the bridges proper began early the next day and continued day and night until completed. The one at Mehrum was 435 metres long and opened for loads up to 40 tons at daylight on 28 March. The longer bridge at Wallach, which stretched for 530 metres, became operational at 0800hrs on 29 March.

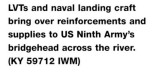

LVTs and naval landing craft bring over reinforcements and supplies to US Ninth Army's bridgehead across the river. (KY 59712 IWM)

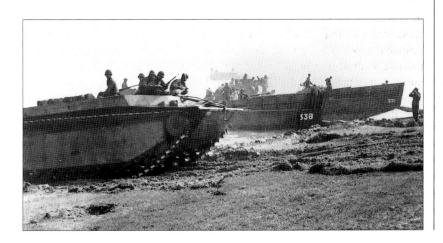

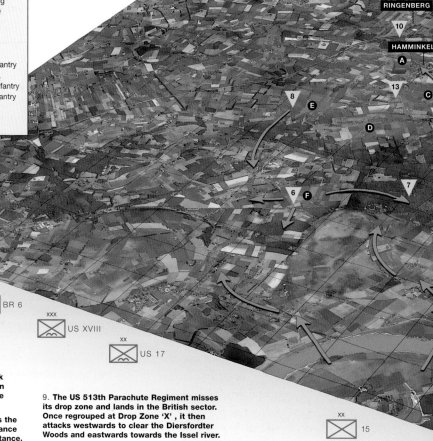

**KEY TO LANDING
AND DROP ZONES:**

A Landing Zone 'O': British 6th Airlanding Brigade with 2nd Ox and Bucks LI 'Coup de Main' Party

B Landing Zone 'U': British 6th Airlanding Brigade with 1st Royal Ulster Rifles 'Coup de Main' Party

C Landing Zone 'R': British 6th Airlanding Brigade

D Landing Zone 'P': British 6th Airlanding Brigade with 6th Airborne Division HQ

E Drop Zone 'B': British 5th Parachute Brigade

F Drop Zone 'A': British 3rd Parachute Brigade

G Landing Zone 'N': US 194th Glider Infantry and 17th Airborne Division's gun area.

H Drop Zone 'X': US 513th Parachute Infantry

I Landing Zone 'S': US 194th Glider Infantry

J Drop Zone 'W': US 507th Parachute Infantry

▼ EVENTS

1. British 1st Commando Brigade attack across the River Rhine at 2200 hours on 23 March and clear Wesel by the middle of the next morning.

2. 15th (Scottish) Division attack across the Rhine at 0200 hours 24 March and advance inland against increasing German resistance.

3. Operation *Varsity* begins at 1000 hours on 24 March. US 1st Battalion 507th Parachute Regiment is dropped 1.5 kilometres to the north-west but soon moves south to the forming-up point.

4. The remainder of US 507th Parachute Regiment drop on target and move to clear the southern part of the Diersfordter Woods.

5. The 3rd Battalion of the American 507th Parachute Regiment capture the village and castle at Diersfordter after a stiff fight.

6. The 8th Battalion, British 3rd Parachute Brigade parachutes in on Drop Zone 'A'. Soon it is joined by the remainder of the brigade to anchor the north-west corner of the airborne lodgement.

7. Canadian 1st Parachute Battalion immediately move southwards through the woods to capture the Schneppenburg feature, overlooking the Rhine.

8. British 5th Parachute Brigade land on Drop Zone 'B' with orders to hold the northern edge of the airborne corps' landings and to seize the crossroads at Mehr-hoog.

9. The US 513th Parachute Regiment misses its drop zone and lands in the British sector. Once regrouped at Drop Zone 'X' , it then attacks westwards to clear the Diersfordter Woods and eastwards towards the Issel river.

10. British 6th Airlanding Brigade with 2nd Ox and Bucks Light Infantry's *coup de main* party arrive in gliders onto Landing Zone 'O' and seize the bridges over the railway and the River Issel between Hamminkeln and Ringenberg

11. A second *coup de main* party from British 6th Airlanding Brigade, the 1st Royal Ulster Rifles, glide down onto Landing Zone 'U' and then take the river bridge east of Hamminkeln.

12. Gliders on Landing Zone 'R' bring in the 12th Devons from 6th Airlanding Brigade with the task of taking Hamminkeln.

13. Landing Zone 'P' provides a base for the remainder of the glider-borne infantry of 6th Airlanding Brigade, the division's guns and the HQ of 6th Airborne Brigade's commander MajGen Bols.

14. Part of US 194th Glider Infantry, the 17th Airborne Division's guns and most of the divisional staff arrive on Landing Zone 'N'. Whilst the area is cleared, a battalion of infantry moves eastwards to seize the line of the River Issel on the flank.

15. The remainder of US 194th Glider Infantry arrive on Landing Zone 'S', and capture a series of bridges over the River Issel.

16. During the early afternoon of 24 March, patrols make contact with the 1st Commando Brigade in Wesel.

17. 1445 hours, 24 March: 6th King's Own Scottish Borderers from British 15th Division join up with US 507th Regiment south of Diersfordt to link together the river and airborne assaults over the Rhine.

OPERATION *VARSITY*: US XVIII AIRBORNE CORPS' ASSAULT EAST OF THE RHINE

Operation *Varsity* was designed to eliminate enemy artillery overlooking the crossing points and to block German movement against the bridgehead. Two airborne divisions, one British and one American, would drop simultaneously on an area north of Wesel in one of the largest airborne operations of the war.

Note: Gridlines are shown at intervals of 1 km (1093 yds)

AIRBORNE LANDINGS

The airborne component of the Rhine crossings was given the code name *Varsity*. It was to be an Anglo-American attack using two airborne divisions of Lt Gen Lewis Brereton's Allied First Airborne Army, British 6th Airborne Division (Maj Gen Bols) and US 17th Airborne Division (Maj Gen William Miley). Brereton assumed that Montgomery would wish British I Airborne Corps (Lt Gen Richard Gale) to command the operation, but was surprised to hear from Twenty-First Army Group's commander that he would prefer US XVIII Airborne Corps under the command of Lt Gen Matthew Ridgway to run the show. The field marshal cited the American's superior signal communications as the main reason, coupled with Ridgway's impressive combat experience. The shortcomings of the British signalling systems at Arnhem was a sensitive matter with Montgomery and he wanted no repetition during the Rhine crossings. Lt Gen Richard Gale was made deputy corps commander for the operation.

On 10 February 1945 a final plan for the deployment of US XVIII Airborne Corps was agreed. Montgomery had insisted that his river crossings be supported by the largest single day's airborne operation of the war in terms of troops, aircraft and gliders. To accomplish this the attack would be delivered the morning after the main attacks across the river had taken place – it was deemed to be more effective to deploy airborne troops in daylight. There was also another good reason for daylight airborne landings. The full weight of all the artillery could be used to support the river assaults without having to avoid any friendly

C-47 Dakota transport aircraft tow gliders of British 6th Airlanding Brigade through a clear sky across France towards their landing grounds on the far side of the Rhine. (CL 2227, IWM)

troops dropping into the target airborne area. It was also hoped that by the time of the drop the enemy would be less likely to anticipate an airborne attack and would be unable to organize a large-scale counter-attack against it because of the scattered nature of the landings. Montgomery also required Gen Ridgway to ensure that the area in which his airborne troops were to operate should be at least within the range of medium artillery. This meant that his landing and drop zones would have to be fairly close to the river.

The employment of US XVIII Airborne Corps in *Varsity* was tactical rather than strategic. Unlike previous airborne operations, it was to arrive after the ground assault had gone in. It was not dropped just to seize and hold ground until relieved, but to take an effective part in the action to establish the Allied lodgement over the Rhine. The main objectives of the corps were to resist enemy counterattacks against the river crossings whilst a bridgehead was being established and to facilitate the advance inland. British 6th Airborne Division was ordered to seize Hamminkeln and the high ground of the Schnepfenberg in the Diersfordter Forest together with the bridges over the Issel river. It was then to link up with British 15th Division and to protect the northern flank of the corps. The American 17th Airborne Division was simultaneously to seize the high ground east of Diersfordt and the bridges over the Issel, then to make contact with 1st Commando Brigade in Wesel and British XII Corps near Bislich in order to link the airborne landings to the river crossings.

To gain these objectives as quickly as possible, each task was subdivided and allotted to smaller groups which were to be landed close to their objectives. The lessons learned from the D-Day and Arnhem operations, where airborne forces had often been landed miles from their objectives, were being put to good effect. It was intended that the two parachute divisions would be put down close enough to their targets to accomplish their tasks immediately after landing, leaving the enemy confused and unable to organize an effective opposition.

The landing area for the airborne attack presented little difficulty for identification from the air. Wesel on the Rhine and the small town of Hamminkeln were obvious landmarks, as were the River Issel, the double-tracked railway from Wesel to Emmerich, the large woodland area of the

The gliders that carried the 2nd Ox and Bucks Light Infantry are scattered across LZ O. In the background the enemy-occupied village of Ringenberg burns furiously. The white outline of the unfinished autobahn runs across the middle of the photo. (BU 2425, IWM)

Airborne troops amongst the wreckage of a glider on the edge of a landing zone near Hamminkeln. (BU 2277, IWM)

Diersfordter Forest and the main road running north from Hamminkeln. British 6th Airborne Division would land paratroopers in two drop zones (DZ-A and DZ-B) and glider-borne troops on four landing zones (LZ-O, LZ-P, LZ-R and LZ-U) all in the north of the airborne bridgehead around Hamminkeln. US 17th Airborne Division would drop into zones in the south of the bridgehead closer to Wesel, with its paratroopers dropping into DZ-X and DZ-W, and its gliders landing on LZ-N and LZ-S.

Varsity was the largest airborne attack of the war flown in one lift. Prodigious numbers of aircraft were required for the operation, both British and American. Gliders carrying British 6th Airlanding Brigade would be towed by RAF Groups 38 and 46; parachute troops would be carried in the C-47 transport aircraft of 52nd Wing of US IX Troop Carrier Command, part of Maj Gen Hoyt Vandenburg's US Ninth Air Force. US 17th Airborne Division would be transported by the other two wings of US Ninth Air Force with the gliders towed by the C-47s of 53rd Troop Carrier Wing and the parachute troops transported in C-46 and C-47 aircraft of 50th Troop Carrier Wing.

Both of the attacking airborne divisions had seen action. The British 6th Airborne was a veteran of the Normandy invasion, having been dropped east of the River Orne the night before the landings. It then remained in the line as infantry for the next two months, before being pulled and reorganized back in England late in August. The US 17th Airborne Division had yet to be dropped in battle. What action it had seen was as infantry during the fighting to stem the German offensive through the Ardennes in December and January.

British 6th Airborne Division was located in England while the US 17th Airborne occupied 12 airfields north and south of Paris. Timings for the fly-in were precise for it would take two hours and 37 minutes for the stream of aircraft carrying these troops to deliver their loads. The two airborne columns would meet over Wavre just to the east of Brussels and fly on parallel courses towards the landing zones. Fortunately, only a few minutes of flying time on the run-in would be over enemy territory. This great air train bringing in the 21,680 paratroopers and glider-borne infantry to the battlefield would comprise 3,933 aircraft and contain 889 escort fighters, 1,696 transport aircraft and 1,348 gliders.

All stages of the *Varsity* operation were to have the safety of an air umbrella overhead. RAF Second Tactical Air Force (2TAF) had final responsibility for fighter cover during the fly-in to the landings. RAF fighter squadrons were to provide air escort of Troop Carrier Command columns from England until they were relieved by 2TAF. US Ninth Air Force was responsible for the air escort of the troop carrier formations from the French airfields until the task was taken over by British 2TAF. Fighters from US Eighth Air Force were to provide a fighter screen east of the landing area during the period of the operation.

Just after 0945hrs on 24 March, the steady drone of hundreds of aircraft began to grow in intensity from the west. All Allied artillery fire along the Rhine stopped. The anti-flak programme aimed at eliminating known enemy anti-aircraft gun positions prior to the airborne assault now halted. The artillery barrage aimed at softening up the Germans still present on the landing grounds had finished 25 minutes previously. All activity on either side of the river came to a halt and all eyes looked skywards to see the vast air armada fly in. Watching the last great airborne operation of the war from a vantage point on a small hill near Xanten were many of the architects of victory: the Supreme Commander Gen Eisenhower, British Prime Minister Winston Churchill, Chief of the Imperial General Staff Field Marshal Sir Alan Brooke and GenFM Montgomery.

BRITISH 6th AIRBORNE DIVISION

At 0710hrs, RAF Stirlings, Halifaxes and C-47s from 38th and 46th Groups began taking off from airfields in East Anglia, towing the 381 Horsa and 48 Hamilcar gliders which were to carry 6th Airlanding Brigade to the Rhine. A short while later, columns of C-47 Dakotas of 52nd Wing of IX Troop Carrier Command were rising from their airfields a little further to the south to begin the task of joining together into one gigantic fleet over Hawkinge in Kent. The flight to the Rhine took just over three hours and at 0945 the formation was approaching its objectives; the silver, snaking line of the great river was clearly visible alongside the plumes of smoke and dust rising from the battlefield.

The leading elements of 3rd Parachute Brigade began to drop at 0951hrs; they were nine minutes early. Enemy flak was light as the initial waves arrived, but intensified as the drop progressed. The pilots of the American C-47 transports dispatched the formation well on target within Drop zone A, in the order 8th Parachute Battalion, Brigade HQ, 1st Canadian Parachute Battalion and then 9th Parachute Battalion. Following the paratroopers, over the next hour or so, came the engineer and medical support units together with an assortment of Horsa and Hamilcar gliders bringing heavier weapons and light transport.

DZ A was situated to the east of the Wesel–Rees road, just to the north of the Diersfordter Forest and near to the village of Mehrhoog.

A group of glider-borne infantry and their transport prepare to move into Hamminkeln. In the centre of the group a German prisoner awaits his fate. (BU 2279, IWM)

The rear end of a British Horsa glider straddles the railway line near Hamminkeln railway station. In the background a party of German prisoners wait to be moved to the rear. (BU 2305, IWM)

The railway station at Hamminkeln. The line, once littered with broken gliders and the gathering point for German prisoners, has now been reduced to a single usable track. (Ken Ford)

The first tasks of 8th Battalion were to clear and secure the drop zone and two areas of woodland on the edge of the forest that jutted into the landing area. As the paratroopers drifted down on their parachutes, enemy fire came at them from these wooded areas. Casualties amongst the paratroopers were light, but gradually increased as more and more men arrived into the drop zone. While the 8th Battalion was trying to establish order, the brigade commander, Brig James Hill, arrived with his headquarters. Next came 1st Canadian Parachute Battalion with orders to capture and clear the south-western corner of the drop zone and then to move into the Diersfordter Forest to seize a feature of higher ground called the Schnepfenberg overlooking the river. Unfortunately, the battalion commander, Lt Col Jeff Nicklin, landed in a tree and was shot dead as he hung in his parachute harness. The 9th Parachute Battalion, arrived a short time later to clear the north and eastern side of LZ A.

All of these tasks were completed during the morning against sporadic German opposition. Some of it was fierce and prolonged, emanating from carefully concealed trench systems and isolated pockets of the enemy. German artillery and anti-aircraft fire proved to be a problem throughout the day, damaging and destroying many of the 30 gliders bringing support services to the brigade which arrived in the late morning. By 1330hrs, however, 3rd Parachute Brigade were masters of the landing ground and had secured the immediate area, anchoring the north-western flank of the corps' sector. The 1st Canadian Parachute Battalion had by then super-imposed itself on the Schnepfenberg feature and sat astride the road from Rees to Wesel. At 1530hrs, a patrol from 3rd Parachute Brigade made contact with the 8th Royal Scots from 15th Division to link up with the river crossings.

The 5th Parachute Brigade descended into DZ B through heavy anti-aircraft fire which shot down two of their C-47 transports on their approach run. Further misfortune hit the American aircraft as they banked away to the west after unloading their passengers. They passed low over the area held by German 7th Parachute Division and were struck by a barrage of fire. Ten aircraft were quickly shot down and seven others were damaged enough for them to have to make crash landings on the way back to the UK.

Brig Nigel Poett and his men jumped onto a landing ground that was criss-crossed with enemy fire. They received a very hostile reception from the Germans holding the area.

They were shot at all the way down, then suffered harassing fire as they struggled out of their parachute harnesses, unfastened their kit bags, extracted their weapons and tried to gather their bearings. It took some time for the three battalions of the brigade to sort themselves out and arrive at their appropriate rendezvous sites. Most casualties were taken during this period. As the paratroopers became more organized, they began to set about the enemy, trying to locate their positions. Once spotted, most groups of the enemy soon capitulated, but those that remained undetected continued to interfere with the landings.

Poett's brigade had the task of screening the northern edge of the airborne corps' landings and securing the road from Hamminkeln to Rees. This it did with its 7th Parachute Battalion along the fields and hedgerows facing north and his 12th and 13th Parachute Battalions astride the Hamminkeln road and the north-eastern edge of the Diersfordter Forest. The brigade's positions were vital to the security of the whole airborne operation and it was onto DZ B that the 4th Airlanding Anti-tank Battery RA landed with its guns. Many of the gliders suffered from enemy flak and landed heavily. Hostile fire made the guns difficult to extract from the broken gliders, slowing down the process of deployment.

The gliders of 6th Airlanding Brigade arrived over landing zones cloaked in smoke. Landmarks so long memorized by glider pilots during training took on a different aspect in the drifting haze. Many pilots were reluctant to cast off their tows until they were sure of their landfall. Exploding anti-aircraft fire and blazing aircraft around them added to the pressure and confusion. Despite all of these diversions, many skilful pilots managed to bring their craft down on or near their target landing zones, others sailed over them into enemy territory or crash-landed in fields and trees.

Leading the brigade's attack were the *coup de main* parties targeted with the tasks of seizing the crossing places over the River Issel and the railway to the east of Hamminkeln. The 2nd Ox and Bucks Light Infantry's gliders landed on LZ O. Although many failed to make the rendezvous point, sufficient men arrived to fight their way through enemy opposition to seize the railroad and river crossings between Hamminkeln and Ringenberg. The remainder of the battalion cut the road north out of Hamminkeln and sealed off the northern edge of the town.

To the south, 1st Royal Ulster Rifles landed on DZ U close by its three main objectives. Again many of the battalion's gliders were damaged by flak and then shot up by enemy machine guns on the ground. Others landed heavily, killing and wounding their occupants. Through all of these setbacks, determined officers and NCOs rallied their troops and one by one secured their objectives. The bridge over the Issel which carried the road east from Hamminkeln was captured intact, as was the level crossing over the rail line. Other parties captured and cleared the area of the station.

The last battalion of 6th Airlanding Brigade, 12th Devonshire Regiment landed on LZ R. Its task was to capture and hold Hamminkeln. This it did in two phases: first, its troops sealed off the town, isolating it from the south and west by seizing the roads to Wesel, Bislich and Rees; next, it staged a full-scale battalion assault on Hamminkeln itself. The garrison in the town by that time were surrounded, some, mostly men from 7th Parachute Division, put up a stiff fight, others capitulated readily. By late afternoon, the town had been completely cleared but was under sporadic enemy shellfire for the rest of the day.

In the centre of 6th Airborne Division's landing grounds was LZ P. This was the destination of Maj Gen Bols' divisional HQ and the landing point of the division's main support units. Horsa and Hamilcar gliders swept onto LZ P throughout the morning, bringing in the pack howitzers of the 53rd Airlanding Light Regiment and the Locust light tanks of the 6th Airborne Armoured Reconnaissance Regiment. Not all of the gliders made it to the landing ground for German flak was now well alerted to the airborne assault, concentrating its fire on the slow-moving gliders and their tug aircraft. Disorientated and confused by the smoke and fire that drifted over the battlefield, many gliders came in too fast or at too steep an angle, crashing into the ground with devastating effect. Of the 24 pack howitzers that set out, only 12 were in action after the landing. The tanks suffered equal losses, with only four of the eight that were dispatched reaching the rendezvous point. By the end of the day only two of these were serviceable.

Maj Gen Bols set up his headquarters in a farmhouse at Köpenhof on the edge of the landing zone, his glider coming to rest just yards from its objective. Within ten minutes his command set was working and the general was in contact with all of his brigades; the link with Maj Gen Ridgway at corps' HQ on the western side of the Rhine was not, however, working, although contact was made with the HQ via the Royal Artillery radio network. Nor was there any direct radio contact with US 17th Airborne, for the British operators dropping with US paratroopers had become casualties.

GLIDER TROOPS OF US 17TH AIRBORNE DIVISION ARRIVING ON LANDING ZONE S, JUST TO THE NORTH-EAST OF WESEL IN THE SECOND DAY OF THE BATTLE.
(Pages 68–69)

The US 17th (*Thunder From Heaven*) Airborne Division, commanded by Maj Gen William Miley, had seen its first combat during the German Ardennes offensive in January 1945. Although elements of the division were flown to Belgium from England in late December 1944 as a lightning response to the massive enemy attack, they were used solely in a ground role as regular infantry. Operation *Varsity*, the airborne component of the Rhine crossings, was the first time that the division fought as a complete formation. The 17th Airborne Division dropped its two parachute regiments, the 507th and 513th Parachute Infantry Regiments, onto drop zones east of the Rhine starting around 0950 hrs on 24 March. The glider borne component of Miley's division, 194th Glider Infantry Regiment, began to arrive on Landing Zones N and S, around 40 minutes later. The airborne operation was unusual in that it took place after the main river assault had gone across and in daylight. Enemy anti-aircraft positions east of the Rhine were still very active and able to put up a veritable wall of flak through which the airborne armada had to fly straight and level while discharging their loads. This great volume of fire disrupted the orderly flights of the aircraft and introduced an element of chaos into the well planned

operation. The scene shows the landings made by the troops of 194th Glider Regiment on Landing Zone S. These men formed the attack arm of the regiment whose objectives were to seize the strategically important five bridges over the River Issel to the east of the landing zone and to link up with British commandos in Wesel. The service element and equipment of the regiment landed a little to the north on Landing Zone N. Unlike the scattered drop of the parachute regiments (1), where paratroopers were strewn over the whole of the US XVIII Airborne Corps' sector in an almost random manner, the gliders were mainly set down on their correct landing zones. The low-flying slow C-47 transports (2) used in the operation for carrying paratroopers and towing gliders became easy targets for enemy anti-aircraft guns and a great number were shot down. Once the glider was released from its tug aircraft the main danger to its safe arrival was from collision with other gliders on the ground. American airborne divisions in the Second World War relied mainly on American built WACO CG-4A gliders (3) to carry their troops, although they did sometimes use the British Horsa type because of its greater carrying capacity. The WACO CG-4A (Hadrian) was a high-wing, boxed-shaped glider capable of carrying 15 fully laden troops. It could also be configured to lift one jeep and six men, or one 75mm howitzer with its five-man crew. The CG-4A was built of wood and metal with much of its exterior covered by fabric. It had a hinged nose that swung upwards to discharge troops or cargo. (4)

US 17th AIRBORNE DIVISION

The 507th Regimental Combat Team was the first of Maj Gen Miley's units to drop. Its aircraft arrived slightly early and the men of the 507th began leaping from their transports at 0950hrs. The C-47 Dakotas came in much lower than the British, with their pilots giving the green light to the paratroopers at an average height of around 200 metres, just high enough for their parachutes to open. This gave them a very short descent and a much better chance of surviving German flak and small-arms fire, but it made the transport aircraft easy targets for enemy fire. Many more were shot down than in the British sector.

The 507th's First Battalion and the regimental HQ led the way down onto what they expected to be Drop Zone W, close to the outskirts of Wesel, but in fact the troops landed about two kilometres to the north-west. Immediately they were on the ground, the Americans were subjected to heavy enemy small-arms fire coming from the Diersfordter Forest to the north. The regiment's commander, Col Edson Raff, and other officers on the ground took some time to get their bearings. After a few moments, Raff decided that they had landed in open fields to the west of the village of Diersfordt. The intended location of the colonel's HQ and the primary objective of the First Battalion lay to the south-east. However, the immediate problem for the paratroopers was the enemy small-arms fire coming from the woods, which was soon supplemented by shellfire from a battery of guns deeper in the forest. The colonel decided

Troops from 44th Brigade of 15th (Scottish) Division link up with paratroopers of 3rd Parachute Brigade to join together the river and air assaults across the Rhine. (BU 2341, IWM)

DZ W just to the north-west of Wesel, the landing ground of the paratroopers of US 507th Parachute Infantry Regiment. The trees lining the far background of the photo are on the southern edge of the Diersfordter Forest. The track up which the regiment's 3rd Battalion advanced on Diersfordt Castle enters the woods in the mid-background. (Ken Ford)

that this had to be silenced first, so he quickly rallied those of his men he could find and led them against the enemy in the trees lining his present landing ground. After a short firefight, Col Raff and his men cleared the Germans from the edge of the woods and eliminated the 150mm gun battery a little farther into the forest, before swinging southwards to attack Diersfordt.

Meanwhile, the Second and Third Battalions of the 507th were descending on the correct landing ground DZ W. The Third Battalion's objective was to capture the village of Diersfordt and its castle. When it had landed and began its advance, the leading troops ran straight into a party of German infantry supported by two tanks which were advancing down a track towards the drop zone. Fortunately, the Americans had with them a new type of gun which was going into action for the first time. The division had been assigned a number of light 57mm recoilless anti-tank guns for the operation and one of these was up with the leading paratroopers. A lucky anti-tank grenade damaged the leading tank. Its crew had surrendered before the first shot from the 57mm gun hit the second tank and set it on fire. The German attack broke up in disorder, withdrawing back into Diersfordt Castle.

By this time Col Raff's party had realized that enemy resistance in Diersfordt was centred on the castle and was planning to attack the fortification; A Company had already been committed to the assault. When his Third Battalion arrived on the scene, Raff decided to leave the castle to them, supported by A Company, and to move the remainder of the 1st Battalion into regimental reserve on the landing ground.

Lt Col Smith led the 3rd Battalion against Diersfordt and its castle in a pincer attack. While two companies laid down a base of fire from the edge of the woods against the upper battlements of the castle, his G Company supported by A Company went at the structure from front and rear. Through a stiff firefight, the Americans fought hard to gain entrance to the courtyard. Once inside, they blew their way into the heart of the castle and began clearing the enemy room by room. It took two hours before the building was totally captured; two hours of close hand-to-hand fighting up spiral staircases, through spacious rooms and across lofty galleries. Pockets of German resistance made a brave last stand at the top of the high turret, eventually having to be blasted from their lofty lair. When it was all over, 300 prisoners filed out of the building, some of whom were senior officers of Gen Straube's LXXXVI Corps and of the 84th Division.

Dropping with the 507th Parachute Infantry Regiment on DZ W was the 464th Parachute Field Artillery Battalion, with its 12 75mm pack howitzers. The gunners came in for a great deal of enemy fire as they struggled in the open to assemble and service their guns, their importance to the attack obvious to the enemy who plastered the area of the landing ground with heavy shellfire. Nine of the guns were in action by 1300hrs and gave aid to the capture of the castle by breaking up German reinforcements moving southwards through the forest towards Diersfordt. As darkness fell the 507th Parachute Infantry Regiment had consolidated its landings, had its guns into position along the edge of the woods overlooking the British 15th Division and had made contact with both that division and the 1st Commando Brigade in Wesel.

Following the drop of Col Raff's regiment came its sister formation, the 513th Parachute Infantry Regiment, commanded by Col Coutts. The majority of its paratroopers were being carried in 52nd Troop Carrier Wing's C-46 Commando aircraft, rather than C-47 Dakotas. The C-46 transport was new to airborne battle and was being used in its first major operation. Faster than the C-47s, the C-46s left their bases after the other aircraft had taken off, expecting to overtake the Dakotas along the route. In the event, the timing was out and they arrived after the leading aircraft of the 507th had dropped.

The pilots completely missed their assigned crossing point over the Rhine and became confused by the smoke and haze and by the heavy flak they met once they had passed the river. It was here that a serious flaw in the aircraft's design revealed itself. The C-46's wing tanks leaked

Diersfordt Castle captured by the 3rd Battalion of 507th Parachute Infantry Regiment on 24 March. The square tower in the centre of the photo was the site of the last stand made by the German troops defending the castle. The building was also the headquarters of some of the staff from both German 84th Division and LXXXVI Corps. (Ken Ford)

The commander of British 6th Airborne Division, Maj Gen Bols, sits at the wheel of his jeep with Brig Hill, commander 3rd Parachute Brigade, alongside of him. (BU 2395, IWM)

fuel into the main body of the aircraft when punctured by shrapnel. It then took just one tracer shell or incendiary to ignite the fuel and the whole aircraft became a flying bomb. In just a few seconds the C-46 could be a mass of flames, plunging earthwards in a spectacular fireball along with its trapped crew and paratroopers.

Flying at less than 200 metres, the C-46s were sitting ducks to German flak and small-arms fire. Nineteen of these aircraft were shot down and a further 38 damaged. As a result of all the confusion, the pilots unleashed their paratroops well away from the designated drop zone. Most of the 513th's men came down in the British airborne's sector, making landfall on the proposed landing ground of the gliders of 6th Airlanding Brigade, three kilometres north of DZ X, where they were supposed to land.

Not surprisingly, there was much confusion amongst Col Coutts's men as they struggled out of their harnesses and came to terms with the enemy fire that raked their landing ground. The flak that had hit the aircraft flying in joined with larger calibre shellfire and small-arms fire to strafe the area. None of the paratroops had the slightest idea as to where they were, nor were they sure in which direction their objectives lay. Several groups gradually formed as officers tried to sort out the mess, even though enemy fire continued to intefere with all movement. Col Coutts was forced to join in with the defence of the landing ground with his own carbine along with the rest of his men. More confusion was to follow when the 2nd and 3rd Battalions of 513th Regiment also landed under fire in another wrong area farther south.

Col Coutts was amazed to see British Horsa gliders now landing amongst his men and increasing numbers of paratroopers with red berets instead of helmets on the landing ground. He naturally assumed that the British had come down in the wrong place. This mistake was rectified when British and American officers consulted each other and got their bearings. Coutts gathered his men around him then set off southwards to the correct forming-up place. When they arrived at DZ X they found the supporting guns of 466th Parachute Field Artillery already in possession. The battalion had made a safe landing earlier onto an almost deserted landing ground, although there had been a considerable amount of enemy fire raking the landing site as it swept in. It was 1230hrs before the regiment had enough men together on their proper site to become an effective force, and 1530hrs before they were on their objectives, some of which had already been taken by men from the 507th.

The glider-borne component of US 17th Airborne Division was the 194th Glider Infantry Regiment, commanded by Col James Pierce. Its leading elements began to arrive at around 1030hrs on two landing zones: LZ N in the north of the division's sector south of Hamminkeln and LZ S just to the north-east of Wesel. Most of the service element of the division landed on LZ N in the north, while those glidermen ordered to seize and hold the five bridges over the River Issel north-east of Wesel and to secure the south-east flank of the airborne assault, landed on LZ S. Success in finding the right landing places was high: 90 per cent of the gliders landed on their correct landing zones.

The experience of the glider-borne infantry of the 194th Regiment was similar to that of the airborne troops on all the other landing and drop zones as enemy flak hit the slow-moving tug aircraft once they crossed the Rhine; German small-arms fire raked the troops and their WACO gliders once they had landed and confusion reigned until experience and training kicked in and order was established. Finally the ground was secured, organized parties attacked objectives and the area gained was eventually consolidated.

Losses were high amongst the WACO gliders and the C-47 transports towing them in. Most of the gliders were ferried in on double tows, the first time this method of using one plane to tow two gliders was used in combat. In total, 610 C-47s towed 906 WACOs. It was successful in practice, but costly when towing C-47s were hit.

Col Pierce's men found the enemy in the south-east corner of the sector a major problem. Attacks of varying strength came at the 194th Regiment throughout the day, mostly by groups from German 84th Division supported by one or two tanks. All were beaten off with considerable loss to the enemy. The bridges over the River Issel were taken and held soon after the landings to secure the eastern flank of the airborne landings and to help facilitate a breakout from the lodgement when the time arose. The British commandos in Wesel were contacted in the early afternoon and the responsibility for the northern flank of Wesel was taken over by the American glidermen.

THE BREAKOUT

The airborne landings had taken the Germans by surprise. Although such an attack had been expected by Commander-in-Chief (West) GenFM Kesselring, all previous Allied airborne operations had been before the main assault. When, on the morning after the night assaults, Kesselring and GenObst Blaskowitz made plans to deal with the night's crossings they did so without the expectation of further landings behind their line. An airborne landing east of the Rhine seemed unlikely. The size and the location of US VIII Airborne Corps' assault when it came left the German commanders with no illusions as to its main objectives. They knew that the airborne troops would try to seize the bridges over the River Issel to help an Allied move inland. Blaskowitz immediately ordered Gen d.Pztrp von Lüttwitz to get across those bridges without delay with the tanks of his XLVII Panzer Corps and to hold them at all costs.

Von Lüttwitz had already begun to deal with the river assaults by ordering his 15th Panzer Division to counterattack the British in Rees and had begun to move some of the tanks and panzer grenadiers from his 116th Panzer Division across to the American side of the Rhine crossings. Some individual tanks were also already in the Diersfordter Forest protecting artillery sites. These were soon engaging American and British paratroopers as they landed. Most of this isolated armour was stalked and knocked out by Allied paratroopers with their anti-tank weapons, other tanks broke out from the enveloping airborne landings to regroup in the north and north-east of the airborne lodgement.

British transport crosses XXX Corps' 'Waterloo' Class 9 folding boat bridge, built downstream of Rees by 18 GHQ Troop's Royal Engineers. It was open to traffic at 0200hrs on 26 March. The bridge classification means that only loads of up to 9 tons are able to use the bridge. (BU 2717, IWM)

The commander of 116th Panzer Division, GenMaj Siegfried von Waldenburg, was now ordered by Von Lüttwitz to make systematic attacks to seize the bridges over the River Issel. Von Waldenburg's men tried, but against dug-in anti-tank guns, concentrated artillery fire from across the Rhine and strafing runs by Allied fighter-bombers, none of their attacks were successful, even though the moves increased in strength towards nightfall. One particular attack against the bridge east of Hamminkeln, however, was partially effective. Tanks and infantry of the 116th Panzer Division came from out of the night at the 2nd Ox and Bucks Light Infantry holding the bridge and almost gained the crossing-place itself. Fearful that great carnage would be done if the German tanks got across and became loose in the rear, the local British commander blew the bridge.

Pressing though the tasks against the airborne were, Blaskowitz later decided that the main threat of a breakout was emerging farther south in US Ninth Army's sector. US 30th Division was making big gains in its advance against 180th Division just south of the Lippe river. Von Waldenburg was soon told to send his 60th Panzer Grenadier Regiment immediately against the Americans and then to follow this with a move southwards of the bulk of his 116th Panzer Division.

Twenty-four hours after the initial waves had crossed the Rhine, FM Montgomery could feel well pleased with the progress that his two armies had made. British Second Army had four divisions and one brigade established on the far side of the river facing the main German force and US Ninth Army had two divisions below Wesel threatening lighter enemy opposition with a breakout. Only on the extreme left of the lodgement around Rees was there any concern.

Earlier that morning the 51st (Highland) Division had lost its commander, Maj Gen Thomas Rennie, killed by mortar bombs whilst on a visit to the tactical HQ of 154th Brigade. He was replaced by Maj Gen MacMillan from 49th Division. The Highland Division had made modest progress throughout 24 March, but had blunted the counterattack by part of Blaskowitz's army group reserve. German 15th Panzer Grenadier

Amphibious Sherman DD tanks from 44th Royal Tank Regiment moving inland to support 15th (Scottish) Division after 'swimming' across the Rhine. All tanks were ashore by 0815hrs on 24 March. (BU 2148, IWM)

American paratroopers of US 17th Airborne Division strike eastwards on the back of a Churchill tank from British 6th Guards Brigade. (BU 2742, IWM)

Division was still preventing the Highlanders moving inland to the north, but villages on either side of the road to Isselburg were falling. Mittelburg and Groin were captured after heavy fighting and the whole of Rees was cleared. Enough space for manoeuvre had now been seized to allow more British formations to be fed into the bridgehead. It was important to Montgomery's plan that Rees and its environs should remain solid against enemy attack. Preparations were now made by Lt Gen Horrocks to feed two more of XXX Corps' divisions into this critical right flank.

The remainder of Canadian 9th Brigade crossed to come under command of 51st Division on 25 March and went on to capture Bienen early on 26 March after an all-night battle. That day XXX Corps' first bridges were completed and 43rd (Wessex) Division began to cross over and advance towards Millingen. Fighting was heavy as 15th Panzer Grenadiers and elements of 7th and 8th Parachute Divisions continued to try to contain the British lodgement. Many hard battles were fought as the veteran Wessex Division pushed hard against the German defenders, capturing Millingen and finally Anholt on 28 March. By this time the 51st Division had Isselburg and the Canadian 3rd Division had crossed over and was advancing westwards towards Emmerich. Also in the bridgehead were the tanks of 8th Independent Armoured Brigade. The pressure being applied to the enemy by three full-strength Allied divisions was irresistible. The already depleted 15th Panzer Grenadier Division and two German parachute divisions gradually succumbed to this pressure, even though they still fought with remarkable skill and bravery, and began to withdraw.

In the centre of British Second Army's front, 15th (Scottish) Division had continued to clear the villages between the river and the airborne landings during 24 March. In the north of its lodgement, 46th and 227th Brigades had captured Mehr and Haffen and were advancing on Mehrhoog and Haldern, despite having to deal with stiff counterattacks by German paratroopers. In the centre, contact had been made with 6th Airborne Division by 44th Brigade at Bergerfurth on the edge of the Diersfordter Forest. Now 157th Brigade from 52nd (Lowland) Division crossed the river and came under command with the task of linking the 15th Division's positions with those of the 6th Airborne.

Early on 25 March, 44th Brigade were ordered to push 16km to the north-east, through the airborne landings, and capture the Wissmann bridge over the River Issel west of Dingen. It was an important mission, for the bridge would form an axis for the forthcoming breakout of the lodgement.

The brigade was led by 6th King's Own Scottish Borderers. They set out at 0730hrs on 25 March, with the two lead companies riding on the back of the tanks of 3rd/4th County of London Yeomanry of 4th Armoured Brigade. The Borderers advanced through 5th Parachute Brigade's positions in the Diersfordter Forest and out across LZ P over land littered with gliders. They were shelled all the way by very active German artillery. This fire slowed the advance down each time it came to any important road or rail crossing for the enemy had the co-ordinates of these places well registered. Beyond theMehr–Hamminkeln road, through DZ B to the unfinished Autobahn, was all open ground. As the tanks moved across the area, they proved to be tempting targets to concealed German anti-tank guns and several of the London Yeomanry's Shermans were knocked out.

The direction of the armoured attack was easily followed by the enemy and when the 6th KOSB arrived near the River Issel they were counterattacked in strength by a fresh battalion of panzergrenadiers supported by tanks. C Company of the Borderers was overrun with its lead platoon wiped out to a man. More tanks arrived to support the Scotsmen and the position was stabilized, though not before the bridge over the Issel was blown by the enemy. The dash to capture the crossing had failed and it was not until early on 27 March that the river barrier was forced and a bridge built.

Back on the Rhine, Lt Gen Ritchie was reinforcing his bridgehead with other formations. The remainder of 52nd Division came into the bridgehead and on 26 March, over the newly completed Class 12 Bailey bridge, the advance elements of 53rd (Welsh) Division crossed and moved up to Hamminkeln. From here they attacked north-eastwards and took Dingen. The next day, 7th Armoured Division crossed the river and moved into the line on the right of the Welsh Division.

Farther south in Wesel, 1st Commando Brigade had spent 24 March clearing out the last of the stubborn enemy from the cellars of the town. The main danger to their hold on Wesel now came from the east where elements of 116th Panzer Division were confronting the American airborne troops along the River Issel. During the day the brigade was reinforced by 1st Cheshires. Later some coloured troops of the American 1698th Engineer Combat Battalion joined in the task of mopping up enemy resistance. They had been ferried over the Rhine with some of their heavy equipment to begin clearing the rubble-strewn streets prior to erecting bridges, for Wesel was to be one of the main

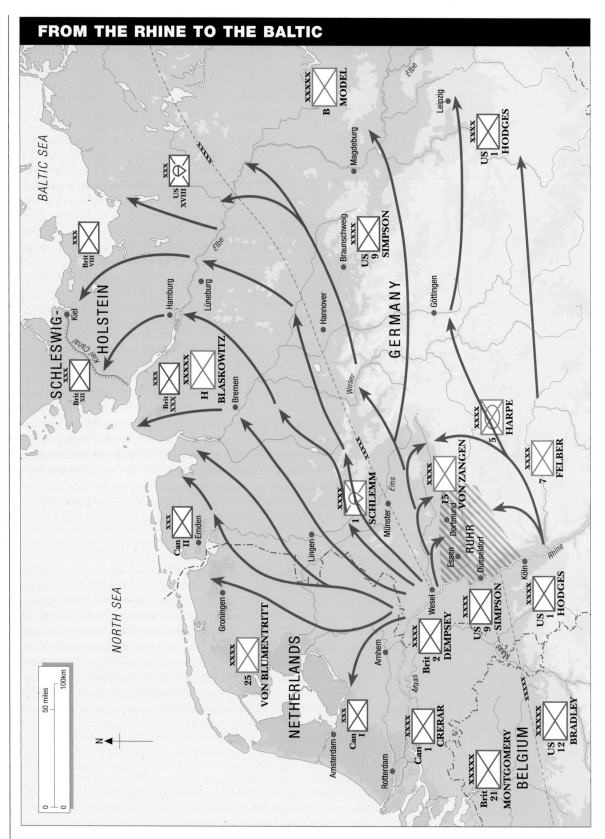

BALTIC SEA

NORTH SEA

GERMANY

NETHERLANDS

BELGIUM

SCHLESWIG-HOLSTEIN

RUHR

XXXXX B MODEL

XXX US XVIII

XXX Brit VIII

XXX Brit XII

XXX Brit XXX

XXXXX H BLASKOWITZ

XXXX US 9 SIMPSON

XXXX US 1 HODGES

XXXX 5 HARPE

XXXX 7 FELBER

XXXX 15 VON ZANGEN

XXXX 1 SCHLEMM

XXX Can II

XXXX 25 VON BLUMENTRITT

XXX Can I

XXXXX Brit 2 DEMPSEY

XXXX US 9 SIMPSON

XXXX US 1 HODGES

XXXX Can 1 CRERAR

XXXXX US 12 BRADLEY

XXXXX Brit 21 MONTGOMERY

Kiel
Kiel Canal
Hamburg
Lüneburg
Bremen
Hannover
Braunschweig
Magdeburg
Leipzig
Göttingen
Münster
Lingen
Emden
Groningen
Arnhem
Amsterdam
Rotterdam
Wesel
Essen
Dortmund
Düsseldorf
Köln

Elbe
Weser
Ems
Rhine
Maas
Maas

50 miles
100km

N

Troops of the 6th King's Own Scottish Borderers move inland from 15th (Scottish) Division's bridgehead. The scattered German dead lying in the open around them suggest that an enemy section had previously been ambushed and slaughtered; their weapons have been removed and the contents of their pockets searched. (BU 2440, IWM)

bridging sites of US Ninth Army. They arrived in the south of the town to find that pockets of the enemy were still active so joined in the task of flushing them out. When the last German in Wesel had finally been captured the next day and the town could at last be declared free of the enemy, the commandos were able to look back on what was a remarkable achievement. The largest town on the Rhine in Twenty-First Army group's sector had been seized with the loss to 1st Commando Brigade of two officers and nine other ranks killed, six officers and 62 other ranks wounded and one officer and 16 other ranks missing. Losses to the enemy were staggering, over 200 dead and 850 captured.

Lt Gen Ridgway's airborne corps spent its first night and the following day holding back enemy counterattacks. It had been resupplied after the assault by 150 Liberator bombers – 15 of which were shot down – and by its own transport columns which were crossing the Rhine in landing craft and Buffaloes. On the first day it could claim to have 109 tons of ammunition, 695 vehicles and 113 artillery pieces deployed on the landing grounds. Soon tanks were being ferried across on Bailey rafts to help stiffen the defence of the landings. British 6th Airborne Division was joined that night with the Churchill tanks of the 3rd Scots Guards from 6th Independent Guards Brigade to help clear the Diersfordter Forest. The responsibility for holding the western flank of the lodgement could now be given over to the formations that had crossed over the Rhine.

On the airborne corps' right flank, US 17th Airborne Division made use of the bridges it had gained over the River Issel and began expanding its territory. The tanks of 116th Panzer Division which had caused some concern the day before had moved farther south to the other side of the River Lippe. Resistance in front of the American paratroopers had eased. By the end of 26 March the division had made a remarkable advance and had pushed almost 10km along the northern bank of the Lippe.

To the south, Lt Gen Bill Simpson could also feel pleased with the progress his XVI Corps had made. Two divisions were well established across the river and bridge building was continuing at an ever increasing pace. On 25 March, both of the assault divisions continued expanding their bridgeheads. The 79th Division had been strengthened by the addition of 134th Regiment from 35th Division and turned the main axis of its attack south-eastwards into the fringe of the Ruhr industrial area. This move brought it into a more densely populated area where progress was inevitably much slower, but it was necessary to make the move to eliminate German artillery positions that were interfering with the bridging sites. Opposition was slight, mainly from small-arms and machine-gun fire from the low-rated Hamburg Division, but occasionally stiffened with airborne troops from 2nd Parachute Division. Meanwhile, the division's 314th Regiment continued with its eastwards advance, moving out into open countryside beyond the second railway line.

Farther north on the morning of 25 March, Maj Gen Hobbs' US 30th Division was moving the last of his artillery battalions across the Rhine ready to support his attack eastwards to seize the line of the unfinished section of autobahn. The attack met only a dispirited defence from German 180th Division which encouraged Hobbs to put together task forces of infantry and armour to strike much deeper into enemy territory. These were quickly assembled by both 117th and 120th Regiments.

The first of these, that of 120th Regiment, began its attack at 1600hrs and immediately ran into much stronger resistance. Little progress was made, but much punishment was inflicted on the Germans who barred its way. The light opposition met earlier in the day from *Volkssturm* units and the remnants of 180th Division had been replaced; the Americans had run into the 60th Panzer Grenadier Regiment from 116th Panzer Division. The battlegroup of the 117th Regiment had not got under way when this news reached it. Hobbs decided on a much more modest objective for the 117th and ordered it to come abreast of the 120th and to hold the line. Further bad news came later that night when 156th Panzer Grenadier Regiment was identified as being in the area. This unit was also from 116th Panzer Division and led Hobbs to believe that the entire Panzer Division was being committed against his sector of the bridgehead. He nonetheless decided that attack was his best option, to prevent the panzer force grouping for its own counterattack.

The bold move paid off, for although few further gains were made during 26 March, much heavy fighting that day blunted Von Waldenburg's tanks and panzergrenadiers moving against the Americans. Honours were even: the 116th Panzers had thwarted an immediate American breakout; the 30th Division had prevented a decisive German counterattack. The stalemate did not, however, last for long. Behind Hobbs' division more formations were crossing the river. The US 35th Division now moved into the area between 30th and 79th Divisions, pushing back the enemy and manoeuvring for more space for even more follow-up divisions. Next to cross was 8th Armoured Division which planned to move through 30th Division and meet tanks with tanks.

GenObst Blaskowitz could not share Montgomery's pleasure over the progress of Operation *Plunder*. The Rhine river barrier had been well and truly broken. Gen d.Fallschirm Alfred Schlemm's First Parachute Army had suffered an attack that had sent it reeling. His II Parachute Corps had performed well, stifling the advance of British XXX Corps, albeit with the help of the 15th Panzer Grenadiers, but by the third day of the battle Meindl's corps was stretched almost to the limit. LXXXVI Corps in the centre had been virtually destroyed. Its 84th Division had disappeared under the weight of a full Allied airborne corps descending amongst it and the 180th Division had been pushed aside by an elite commando brigade and by two American divisions. In the south, Gen d.Inf Erich Abraham's LXII Corps, never a formation with great offensive spirit, containing as it did the motley collection of *Volkssturm* units that made up the Hamburg Division, had been overwhelmed by a single American division. Blaskowitz knew that an attempt to hold the Rhine could not now be successful.

With the battle for the bridgehead seemingly won, Montgomery's battle for the breakout could now begin. But first, the key to this second battle, the erection of sufficient bridges to carry three armies eastwards, had to be given top priority. Bridging operations on British Second Army's front were slow, subjected as they were to much larger concentrations of German artillery than the Americans. By the end of the day on 26 March, US Ninth Army had four bridges in operation in addition to the two they had completed at Wesel. The bridges at Wesel, however, although destined to be the main crossing places for the American drive east along the roads which radiated from the town, were under temporary British control and only available to Simpson's men for five hours a day. The remainder of the time they were desperately needed by Second Army to supply its lodgement.

The first of the British Class 40 Bailey bridges on XXX corps' front, 'London Bridge', opened for traffic at midnight on 26 March. Prior to this, a Class 9 and a Class 15 bridge had been completed earlier that morning. The remaining two Class 40 Baileys, 'Blackfriars' and 'Westminster' Bridges, were ready for use on 27 and 28 March respectively. All of these bridges were built in the vicinity of Rees. XII Corps' first bridge, a Class 9 folding boat bridge, was open for light traffic just before midnight on 25 March. Later two Baileys, one a Class 12 and one a Class 40, were built on the river next to Xanten. Across these large Bailey bridges now passed the transport and armour required for the breakout.

Three days after the initial assaults, the bulk of four Allied corps gathered west of the Rhine preparing to cross the river and exploit the breakout when it came. On 27 March, the German line began to buckle under the inexorable weight being applied by Montgomery's two armies. Many extra formations had joined in the battle. On the left, XXX Corps had put the 3rd Division across the river into the right-hand sector of the corps' line. Soon after, the Guards Armoured Division traversed the Bailey bridges at Rees and joined in the action. In the centre, XII Corps had further reinforced its bridgehead with the infantry tanks of the 34th Independent Armoured Brigade. To the south, US XVI Corps had put its fifth infantry division across the Rhine when 75th Division moved into the right-hand sector of the line.

Montgomery now began to implement the breakout phase of the operation. Late on 27 March, he issued directives to his three army commanders. He intended to exploit the rapidly deteriorating German

ROYAL ENGINEERS BUILD THE FIRST BAILEY BRIDGE OVER THE RIVER RHINE IN BRITISH XXX CORPS' SECTOR, JUST UPSTREAM OF REES. (Pages 84–84)

The first major British Bailey bridge to be completed across the River Rhine was at Rees and was built by 8th GHQ Troop Royal Engineers, part of 13th Army Group Royal Engineers. The bridge, code named London, was begun at 1700 hrs on 25 March and completed at 2300 hrs on 26 March. It was the first of two Bailey bridges at Rees, sited to make good use of the network of roads that radiated out from the town on the enemy side of the river. London bridge (1) was a low level Bailey, 1,174 feet in length, built to allow for a four-metre variation in water level. It was constructed from sections of metal panels (2) fixed to floating bays (3). These bays were assembled at the water's edge on either side of the Rhine and towed out into the river to be bolted together to form a continuous roadway. At either ends, sloping landing bays (4) connected the bridge to the shore. All military bridges were given a load classification number so that drivers using the crossing could know if the structure was capable of carrying the weight of their vehicles. This classification number was shown at the entrance to the bridge by a white disc with red lettering. The Bailey bridge at Rees was a Class 40 (5) construction, which meant that it

could carry loads of up to 40 tons – tanks and fully loaded trucks could cross, but not loaded tank transporters. After an assault, the first bridge to be constructed was usually a Class 9 folding boat bridge which was often started within hours of the infantry making the initial assault. This type of bridge was quick to build and would allow carriers, anti-tank guns and light transport to get over into the lodgement formed by the infantry. When the enemy had been cleared right away from the bridging site, construction of the stronger Bailey bridges could begin. Usually this work was not interfered with by enemy small arms fire, but almost always it was subjected to long-range artillery fire, once the enemy had identified the crossing place. One of the most useful pieces of equipment that sappers possessed was the bulldozer (6). They were the first machines to begin work on any bridging site, clearing the area and constructing a ramp down to the river. They were also always on call by the leading infantry for a variety of tasks, ranging from pushing aside roadblocks to filling in craters and bulldozing by-passes around obstructions. Casualties to engineers manning these machines were often high, for the urgent need for the leading troops to get ahead resulted in the bulldozers being right up at the front and the noise they generated often brought down a deluge of enemy fire.

resistance and to drive hard eastwards for the River Elbe so as to gain command of the open plains of northern Germany. First Canadian Army would open up a supply route to Arnhem and then clear north-west Holland and the coastal belt. In the centre, British Second Army would be directed on Hamburg. In the south, US Ninth Army's advance would be twofold: its left would head for Magdeburg on the Elbe, whilst its right would help US First Army clear the Ruhr industrial area.

The next day Montgomery received news that his orders had been changed by the Supreme Commander. Eisenhower directed that once Simpson's Ninth Army had reached Paderborn, it was to revert to the command of Gen Bradley as part of Twelfth Army Group. The main advance through Germany would now be made in the centre by Bradley's army group, directed through Erfurt and Leipzig to Dresden, with Montgomery's British Second Army acting as a flank guard. These changes no longer made Berlin the main Allied objective as had been previously agreed. Eisenhower now saw the German capital as nothing more than a 'geographical location', one that was being left to the Russians to capture.

On 28 March, XII and XXX Corps continued to make steady progress, although resistance on the left from the German parachute infantry and the panzer grenadiers was still strong. XII Corps had expanded its front to contain three infantry and one armoured division. The 53rd Division, supported by 4th Armoured Brigade, attacked through 52nd Division northwards from Ringenberg to Bocholt breaking open the German resistance in front of XII Corps. The 7th Armoured Division with 157th Brigade under command took advantage of the confusion and advanced towards Borken. Progress was good, but even greater moves were under way on the right of the armoured division.

VIII Corps was now activated and its 11th Armoured Division crossed the Rhine on the right of Second Army. The remainder of its 6th Independent Guards Brigade had also moved over the river and come into the small section of the line still held by US XVIII Airborne Corps. The Guards Brigade's Churchill tanks, not the fastest of armour, were placed at the disposal of the airborne divisions for the breakout. The American 17th Airborne Division mounted the Churchills of the 4th Coldstream and 3rd Scots Guards at mid-afternoon on 28 March and moved off. After a short struggle through the enemy line, the columns roared forward, heading for Dorsten. It was a spectacular advance and by the end of the day the Americans had raced 28 kilometres to a point to the north of the town. The next day it reached Haltern. Its effect was far reaching, for the advance had outflanked the positions of German XLVII Panzer Corps in contact with US 30th Division to the south. Lüttwitz had no choice but to pull back and try to realign his 116th Panzers. The turn of the British 6th Airborne Division came the next day when its paratroopers made an equally impressive move to the east, mounted on the tanks of the 4th Grenadier Guards.

The advance of the airborne troops and the gathering strength of US XVI Corps caused the German line to falter. US 30th Infantry and 8th Armoured Divisions continued to batter away at enemy forces south of the Lippe, but noticed that their efforts were bringing greater results. On 29 March Gen Simpson announced a plan for the next phase of the breakout. Maj Gen Anderson's XVI Corps would swing south-eastwards

EXPANDING 21ST ARMY GROUP'S BRIDGEHEAD, 24–28 MARCH 1945

After a bridgehead had been secured over the River Rhine on 24 March, FM Montgomery gradually increased Allied concentrations. By 28 March the German defences were so stretched that they broke and Montgomery's forces stepped up their drive eastwards.

Note: Gridlines are shown at intervals of 5 km (3.10 miles)

EMMERICH
18

KALKAR
REE
1

XAN

xx
3 CAN

xxx
II CAN

xx
43

xx
51

xx
3

xxx
XXX BR

xx
15

xxx
XII BR

xx
53

xx
BR 6

xx
7

xx
XVIII US

xxx
XVI US

xx
17 US

xx
35 US

8 US

xx
79 US

xx
30 US

▼ EVENTS

1. **British XXX Corps opens the attack with the crossing of 51st (Highland) Division at 2100 hours on 23 March.**

2. **British XII Corps attacks at 2200 hours, with 1st Commando Brigade crossing to seize Wesel.**

3. **British XII Corps continues its assault at 0200 hours on 24 March with a crossing by 15th (Scottish) Division.**

4. **US XVI Corps opens US Ninth Army's attack at 0200 hours with a crossing by its 30th Division upstream from Wesel**

5. **An hour after 30th Division's crossings, US XVI Corps launches its 79th Division across the Rhine at 0300 hours.**

6. **Early on 24 March, Gen Blaskowitz releases German Army Group B's reserves and confronts British landings at Rees with the 15th Panzer Grenadier Division from XLVII Panzer Corps.**

7. **At 1000 hours on 24 March, US XIII Airborne Corps begins landing British 6th and US 17th Airborne Divisions. They seize bridges over the River Issel and link up with 1st Commando Brigade in Wesel and the landings of 15th (Scottish) Division.**

8. **25 March: US 30th Division overcomes counterattack by German 116th Panzer Division.**

9. **26 March: MajGen Anderson deploys US XVI Corps' armour and orders 8th Armored Division to breakout eastwards south of the River Lippe.**

10. **26 March: US XIII Airborne Corps hands over its left flank to British XII Corps and then advances towards the Shermbeck-Erle line on the tanks of British 6th Guards Brigade, trying to manoeuvre a breakout.**

11. **15th (Scottish) Division attack northwards during 25 and 26 March against heavy enemy opposition.**

12. **51st (Highland) Division battles against the strongest German counterattacks by 15th Panzer Grenadiers and reaches Isselburg. The enemy start to withdraw.**

13. **26 March: US 35th Division crosses the Rhine to secure the inner flanks of 30th and 79th Divisions as the bridgehead expands.**

14. **26 March: US 79th Division swings south-eastwards towards the Ruhr industrial area and is met by weak counterattacks from German 2nd Parachute Division.**

15. **27 March: XII Corps introduces 53rd (Welsh) Division into the battle and orders it to take Dingden.**

16. **XII Corp's armour, the 7th Armoured Division, arrives on 27 March and attacks through Brunen.**

17. **27 March: XXX Corps introduce 43rd (Wessex) Division on the left flank of 51st Division to help push back the now faltering 15th Panzer Grenadier Division.**

18. **Canadian 3rd Division crosses the Rhine on 28 March and advances to take Emmerich. All along the line the enemy is falling back. Montgomery's breakout to the east has begun.**

XX ☒ 364

XX ☒ 6

XX ☒ 15

XX ☒ 8

XXX ⬭ XLVII

XX ⬭ 116

XX ☒ 7

XXX ☒ II

XXX ☒ LXXXXVI

XX ☒ 84

6

12

11

7

15

16

2

WESEL

4

10

DINSLAKEN

8

9

5

RIVER RHINE

14

13

DORTMUND-EMS CANAL

DUISBURG

ESSEN

XX ☒ 180

XX ☒ Hamburg Division

MULHEIM

XXX ☒ LXIII

XX ☒ 2

N

to build a line on the Rhein–Herne Canal on the northern edge of the Ruhr. Maj Gen McLain's XIX Corps would now cross the Rhine to take over the main effort, moving eastwards along the line of the Lippe with two armoured and three infantry divisions. It would then swing slightly to the south against the north-eastern tip of the Ruhr. US Twelfth Army Group would attack the southern side of the Ruhr with Hodges' US First Army and also send a corps to meet McLain's formation at Paderborn, thus totally encircling the great Ruhr industrial region. Simpson's other corps, Maj Gen Alvan Gillem's XIII Corps, would cross the river at Wesel once the British had released command of the bridges and drive eastwards. At that time, US XVIII Airborne Corps would be relieved, with the American units joining XIII Corps and the British units reverting to their VIII Corps.

In the north, the slogging match around Rees between the men of British XXX Corps and the enemy paratroopers and panzer grenadiers continued. The local initiative had now passed well and truly to Lt Gen Horrocks' corps and great gains were made all along this line, seizing much needed elbow room through which to pass the gathering weight of the corps. On 30 March, XXX Corps broke out of the bridgehead with the Guards Armoured Division in the lead. Horrocks' formation was to act as flank guard to the other two corps of British Second Army as they carried the main effort to the River Elbe. XXX Corps was headed towards Bremen and the mouth of the Elbe.

On XXX Corp's left, Canadian II Corps captured Emmerich and drove north against negligible resistance, heading for the north of Holland and the German cities of Emden and Wilhelmshaven on the coast. On its left, Canadian I Corps moved down the Rhine towards Arnhem and the centre of Holland.

The positioning of VIII and XII Corps meant that they would carry the main thrust of Montgomery's move eastwards, with XII Corps heading for the great port of Hamburg and VIII Corps for the Elbe beyond Lüneburg. Some reorganization of the two formations was made to equalize their

Guns from one of Second Army's medium artillery regiments cross over the Rhine on a newly completed Bailey bridge. (BU 2392, IWM)

strength. Lt Gen Barker's VIII Corps now had under command 11th Armoured, 6th Airborne and 15th (Scottish) Divisions, 1st Commando Brigade and 6th Guards Armoured Brigade. Lt Gen Ritchie's XII Corps contained 7th Armoured, 52nd and 53rd Divisions, and the 4th Armoured Brigade. The 3rd Infantry Division joined the corps later.

Set free from the confines of the bridgehead, Allied forces everywhere began a great advance. Within just a few more days, the front line had been pushed back 100 miles from the river. Rapid advances were made everywhere against an enemy who was now only capable of delaying actions and half-hearted counterattacks. Operation *Plunder* had been a success and Montgomery had won his last great battle; the river barrier of the Rhine had been crossed and Allied forces had been set free across northern Germany. It was the beginning of the end for the Nazi regime. Six weeks after the Rhine crossings, Hitler was dead and Germany had capitulated.

The scale of Operation *Plunder* was truly impressive, in terms of the numbers of men and the quantity of matériel involved. In many ways it rivalled the Normandy invasion in size and scope. Although high in cost, it was, comparatively speaking, not great in human tragedy. Losses were modest when considering the numbers of men that took part. British Second Army's casualties up to 27 March were 3,968; US Ninth Army's total was 2,813. Over 16,000 enemy prisoners were taken.

Many historians have criticized the scale of Operation *Plunder*, likening it to taking a sledgehammer to crack a nut. American crossings farther to the south were accomplished with only a fraction of the resources available to Montgomery. We must remember that the Rhine crossings had been planned when the river was seen as a greater barrier than it actually was. The planned concentration of strength was organized before the German Army Group H was decimated in the Rhineland battles to the west of the river. If Hitler had withdrawn his best units behind the Rhine in February, then it would have needed all of Operation *Plunder*'s power to make the crossing. With all the resources available to him, it would have been amiss of Montgomery not to have used them when he made his assault.

There is one part of the operation, however, that invites even more criticism, the use of US XVIII Airborne Corps after the initial crossings. The American official history of the campaign questions whether the airborne attack was necessary or even justified. It cites the particularly weak condition of the German units on the far side and the vulnerability of airborne units and aircraft in daylight whilst the drop is made. It makes a sound point, for, although the airborne landings were successful, most of the objectives taken could most likely have been captured by ground troops at much less cost. They were after all just a few kilometres from the river, and the bridges over the Issel that were thought to be so vital could each have been replicated with just one span of Bailey bridge. The river was just 20m wide and easily fordable by troops on foot. Casualty figures seem to illustrate the point: 17th Airborne Division losses on the first day were 159 men killed, 522 wounded and 800 missing. IX Troop Carrier Command lost 41 killed, 153 wounded and 163 missing. The airborne assault cost over 50 gliders and 44 transport aircraft destroyed and 332 damaged. Fifteen Liberator bombers were lost over the battlefield.

THE BATTLEFIELD TODAY

The ground over which the Rhine crossings by British Twenty-First Army Group took place have been cleared of all traces of battle and returned to more peaceful use. The area is now mostly arable farmland. Towns and villages are still of modest size, save for those in the south near the Ruhr. German industry there is concentrated in urban areas and is still churning out manufactured goods, just as it did when it was servicing the Nazi war effort.

Along the Rhine valley the river runs deep and wide, quietly passing the crossing places so alive in 1945. The waterway is once again a busy thoroughfare, carrying a continuous stream of barges to and from North Sea ports into the heart of Germany. The derelict brick viaduct leading to the old rail bridge at Wesel still stands, the last vestige of all the pre-war bridges over the Rhine: all present bridges across the river are now post-war. Few other man-made structures of 1945 vintage remain, save for the houses not caught up in the fighting. The main interest in visiting the area is to see the locations where the events happened.

The crossing places of US Ninth Army lie to the south of Wesel. Most of the actual sites where the assaults took place are not easily accessible by car, for the shifting Rhine and frequent flooding has ensured that the roads lie well back from the river. A good view of the stretch of river crossed by US 30th Division can be obtained from the waterfront at Buderich. On the far shore most of the villages are still intact in an area where the fighting was relatively light. The town of Dinslaken has grown considerably, as have the areas to the south which touch the edge of the Ruhr industrial region.

On the western end of the Wesel road bridge are the remains of the nineteenth-century Fort Blücher, its ramparts cut by the ramp feeding the bridge. The fort was the refuge of the last few Germans who remained west of the river when their line of retreat was cut after the bridge was blown. The pockmarked walls of the fort give witness to the last stand put up by the abandoned enemy soldiers who finally succumbed to US Ninth Army troops on 11 March. Most of the fort was demolished 17 days later by American engineers to provide rubble for approach roads to their Bailey bridge.

Wesel has been completely rebuilt after its devastation by heavy bombers of the RAF. The town's Gothic church has been completely restored with its spire once again rising above the flowing Rhine. The pockmarked granite pillars of the eastern side of the old rail bridge now form a viewing platform with good views downriver towards the crossing place of British 1st Commando Brigade. A short distance to the north is the area where the 1st Cheshires landed early on 24 March to support the commandos.

The 10,000 metre marker stone on the banks of the Rhine at Bislich, placed in 1867 as one of the 65 distance stones along the length of the river from the North Sea to its source. The bullet securely imbedded in its face shows signs of 15th (Scottish) Division's action that took place nearby. (Ken Ford)

Farther downstream almost the whole of the Grav Insel, where the commando brigade crossed the Rhine, is now a large caravan park. Leading down to the river along NATOstrasse, is a modern concrete road built by the German Army. The area along the river here is used as an amphibious training ground and solid ramps now lead down to the water where 46 RM Commando's Buffaloes struggled ashore. The patched-up walls of the strongly defended 'waterman's cottages' taken by the commando still stand, now surrounded by the cages of the caravan park's small family zoo.

Just a little to the north is the landing ground of US 507th Parachute Regiment, crossed by a road leading north-west directly to the village and castle of Diersfordt. The castle is more a stately home than a fortress, but it took the American parachutists almost a day of battle to capture it. The fighting went from room to room, until a last stand by the enemy was made in its high tower. Evidence of this life and death struggle can be seen on the walls outside. Across the road from the castle is Diersfordt German war cemetery. Tucked away on the edge of the Diersfordter Forest are the graves of 385 German soldiers, almost all of whom were killed during the first two days of the battle.

The area west and north of Diersfordt is covered with newly formed lakes, the by-product of much sand and gravel extraction in the region. The crossing places of 15th Scottish Division were mainly to the north of Bislich, with the 6th Royal Scots Fusiliers landing directly in front of the village. To the north-west, on the edge of the Diersfordter Forest is DZ A, the landing site of British 3rd Parachute Brigade with the slightly higher ground of the tree-covered Schnepfenberg feature a little farther to the south. Between the two runs the road towards Hamminkeln. The 6th King's Own Scottish Borders advanced on the back of the tanks of the 3rd/4th County of London Yeomanry, through the airborne landings, to attempt to seize the Wissmann bridge over the River Issel west of Dingen. The road runs across the main glider landing ground of British 6th Airborne Division, LZ P, with the American LZ N a little farther to the south.

At Hamminkeln the bridges over the River Issel seized in two *coup de main* attacks by the 2nd Ox and Bucks Light Infantry and 1st Royal Ulster Rifles, have been replaced. The river here looks to have been straightened and its banks squared off leaving no more than a deep stream, belying the great efforts taken to seize these strategic crossing places. The railway here is reduced to a single track and the station at Hamminkeln is no more than a little-used halt. By the station is a rare oddity in Germany, a memorial to the men of the 52nd Light Infantry, the Ox and Bucks, who took the area by force and killed many Germans in the process. One wonders if such a monument to the deeds of a modern invading force would be tolerated in Britain or the USA today.

BIBLIOGRAPHY

Allen, Peter, *One More River*, J.M. Dent, London (1980)

Anon, *Airborne Forces*, The Air Ministry, London (1951)

Anon, *By Air To Battle*, HMSO, London (1945)

Anon, *The Story of 79th Armoured Division*, Privately Printed, Hamburg (1945)

Ellis, Maj L. F., *Victory in the West Volume II*, HMSO, London (1968)

Essame, Maj Gen H., *The 43rd Wessex Division at War 1939–1945*, William Clowes, London (1952)

Essame, Maj Gen H., *The Battle For Germany*, Batsford, London (1969)

Ford, Ken, *The Rhineland 1945*, Osprey, Oxford (2000)

Graves, Charles, *The Royal Ulster Rifles*, Royal Ulster Rifles Regimental Committee, York (1950)

Harclerode, Peter, *'Go To It': the Illustrated History of 6th Airborne Division*, Caxton Editions, London (2000)

Macdonald, Charles B., *The Last Offensive*, Center of Military History, Washington DC (1951)

Martin, Lt. Gen. H.G., *The History of the Fifteenth Scottish Division*, William Blackwood, Edinburgh (1948)

Mitchem, Samuel W., *Hitler's Legions*, Leo Cooper, London (1985)

Montgomery, Field Marshal Bernard, *Normandy to the Baltic*, Hutchinson, London (1947)

Montgomery, Field Marshal Bernard, *Memoirs*, Collins, London (1958)

Mrazek, James E., *The Glider War*, Robert Hale, London (1975)

Norton, G.G., *The Red Devils*, Leo Cooper, London (1971)

Salmond, J.B., *The History of the 51st Highland Division*, William Blackwood, Edinburgh (1953)

Stacey, Col C.P., *The Canadian Army 1939–1945*, Ministry of National Defence, Ottawa (1948)

Stacey, Col C.P., *The Victory Campaign Volume II: Operations in North-west Europe 1944–1945,* The Queen's Printer and Controller of Stationery, Ottawa (1960)

St George Saunders, Hilary, *The Green Beret*, Michael Joseph, London (1949)

Weigley, Russell F., *Eisenhower's Lieutenants*, Sidgwick & Jackson, London (1981)

Whiting, Charles, *Bounce the Rhine*, Casemate, Pennyslvania (2002)

INDEX